LEARN

LIBRARY AND SOCIETY

Dr. Anil Kumar Dhiman

and

Smt. Yashoda Rani

Ess Ess Publications

4837/24, Ansari Road, Darya Ganj,
New Delhi-110002
✆ : 23260807
Fax : 23274173
E-mail: info@essessreference.com
url:http://www.essessreference.com

First Published 2005

ISBN : 81-7000-446-2

Price : 250/-

Published by :

Ess Ess Publications

4837/24, Ansari Road, Darya Ganj,
New Delhi - 110 002
Phone : 23260807
Fax : 23274173
E-mail: info@essessreference.com
url:http://www.essessreference.com

Printed at :

Printline, New Delhi

Contents

Learning Library Science Series

Each book in this series has been written to provide in-depth knowledge of the basics of Library and Information Science and is in accordance with the B.Lib.Sc. syllabus of major Indian universities imparting the said course. To make this work series more comprehensible for the students, the books under this series have been written in Question-Answer format and the language used is very simple, easy and understandable. This series has been divided into six parts, each of which is dedicated to one basic aspect of library and information science.

The present series consists of six books in all, its first part deals with Learn Library and Society, second is Learn Library Management, third is Learn Library Classification (Theory), fourth being Learn Library Classification (Theory), fifth, Learn Reference Services, Information Services and Their Sources and the last and sixth book is Learn Computer Basics and its Application in Libraries. This gives a comprehensive and complete coverage to almost all the syllabi of most of the Indian universities imparting Bachelors' Degree in Library and Information Science (B.Lib.Sc.).

Although this book has primarily been written, keeping in mind the students making an attempt at the above mentioned Degree course, but it is hoped that this book shall find its place with anyone who is interested to know and learn more about the basics of library and information science. Not only the students, but the teachers of library and information science can derive equal benefit from this series. The books are equally suited to librarianship, library science students and library staff seeking to upgrade their skills.

Authors

Acknowledgements

It is indeed difficult to write one book and writing such a series of books is naturally much more difficult but this series could finally see the light of the day, but this could never have been possible without those innumerous books which have been consulted at every step and we are grateful to the authors of all those books, naming all of whom would not be humanly possible. We are thankful to Mrs. Sheel Sethi and Mr. Sumit Sethi, the owners of Ess Ess Publications for giving us an opportunity to present this voluminous work to the readers. We would also like to record our thanks to our friend, Mr. Sushil Kumar of IIT, Roorkee for his kind help. We feel indebted to Sh. Ram Lal Dhiman, Smt. Kamla Devi and Ms. Alka Rani who helped us at various steps. Last but not the least, we are thankful to our son Aman who could not get much of our attention while we were working on this work.

Anil. K. Dhiman
Yashoda Rani

1

Library, Its Growth and Development and Role in Modern Society

Q. : Describe the history and developments of libraries.

or

Define the concept of library and discuss its developmental history with particular reference to India.

Ans. : The word library which in English refers to a collection of books gathered to study, research, reference and recreation, is derived from the Latin *Libra* meaning a book. But the word *Libraire* in French does not have the same meaning and is used to denote a bookshop or, by extension, publisher. The word *Bibliotheca* in Greek is also used to signify a collection of books ; *bibliotheque* in French, *biblioteca* in Italian *bibliothek* in Germany and *biblioteka* in Russian are also used for the same.

As far as, its Hindi name *Pustakalaya* is concerned, it itself is self explanatory; consisting of

Pustak = Book

Aalaya = the house

As such the house of books stands for *Pustakalaya* or the library.

The library word is used to denote a building, room or set of rooms in which a collection of books is housed. Hence, the library is represented as a trinity of :

— Books
— Readers and
— Staff

More appropriately said, a library housed an organized collection of documents to preserve them and make available for use.

Concept and Development of Library

When we talk about the origin of libraries, it is very difficult to say when the first library was set up . But it can be supposed that when the man started to use the writing media as the communication medium, and started to collect them for future retrieval, the ides of a library could be originated.

By about 2,500 BC, the Egyptians had discovered a very satisfactory and relatively cheap writing material, *papyrus*, made from the sedges which grew along the banks of the Nile. This is the substance from which our modern word, paper, derives its name and its cellulose fibre base also constitutes the chemical base for most modern papers. Some proofs of libraries are observed around 3 BC in ancient Alexandria. In ancient Mistra sacred places, some records reveal the existence of libraries at that time. There are the proofs of libraries during Asyria Babylon culture, where during 668-626 BC, the books were kept in a very systematic ways according to their subjects. The *Mudranls* were used to determine the places of books and the catalogues of books were also prepared.

About 105 AD paper more akin to that in present use was being produce by the Chinese but the technique which they used did not reach Western Europe till about 1150 AD. In the meantime the Barbarian successors to the Roman empire had to make do with hides and skins, e.g. parchment (sheep-skin) or vellum (calf-skin) which could be prepared and treated to provide extremely good and very durable writing material, but at the expense of a great deal of time and effort , so book-production, and hence libraries-creation, became slow and costly. By 1280, paper was being produced in Italy and its use spread rapidly throughout Europe. However, it still had to be written on by hand. Records, deeds and other documents were still kept in the form of rolls, though from about 100 AD, books had been produced in the form of leaves bound between wooden boards, usually covered in leather. Such books are known as codices (singular - codex), the Greek word for a block of wood, which they somewhat resembled in outward appearance. But as was said above, they were written by hand i.e., in manuscript.

In the early Christian era, the Chinese had also invented a form of printing - block-printing - by engraving characters on blocks of wood, inking these and impressing them upon paper. A remarkable example is a Buddhist charm which a Japanese empress caused to be printed in this fashion in 770 AD, in no less than 100,000 copies, and distributed throughout her country in an attempt to ward off an epidemic. In about 1030 AD, the Chinese took a step further by printing from movable type, i.e., one character to a block. This process, however, was unknown to the world beyond the far east until, round 1440 AD, at Mainz, in Germany, Johann Gutenberg and his associates began to produce books, using a similar method. Multiple copies of letters of the alphabet were cast in metal. These were made up in a suitable frame to form words and sentences. This type was locked into the bed of a press inked, a piece of paper was placed over it and it was then rolled under a heavy weight, the platen, which was pressed down upon the paper, so transferring to it in ink the image of the type. From then on, the existing principal 'container' of information, the manuscript book gave way to the printed book, which in its earliest swaddling bands' incunabula state looked like a codex (rather as the earliest cars looked something like the carriages which they superseded) but which by about 1600 had most of the attributes title page, content list, page-numbers, etc. of the modern book.

Printing spread from Germany to Italy, the Netherlands, France, England and so back through Asia and to the 'new worlds' as they were found and conquered by the merchant-marauders of western Europe. It is interesting to note that the art and craft of printing spread through Europe just at the right time to be useful in the biggest upheaval of thought since the days of classical Greece; the time of the flowering of the great split in Christendom caused by the protesting would-be reformers of what these considered to be abuses of power by the Roman Catholic church. In 1517, Martin Luther started it with his great written statement which he nailed to the door of Wittenberg cathedral. The long bloody and atrocious wars of national politics and religion began and the protagonists fought, not only with sword and cannon, but also with tongue, with pen and with print. Instant publication was achieved by the production of single sided broad sheets and paper-covered loose-sewn tracts and lampoons pamphlet literature. By 1700, with the wars of religion and nationality dying down and the growth of urban civilization centred upon national capital cities newspapers were produced and also learned journals which contained accounts to the proceedings of and papers read before, the new philosophical, literary and scientific societies. The Industrial Revolution starting in England around 1750, and the political revolutions in the U.S.A and France, in the last quarter of the eighteenth century gave rise to an ever-greater demand for debate, free discussion, 'know-how' and education and so for information and the tools with which to mine it - reading and writing- and for containers and stores for it books and libraries. By 1800, paper was being made by steam-driven machinery and by 1820 steam-driven presses were in use. By 1900, new receptacles for information had been developed: the photograph, the slide the film, the sound recording. By the 1950s the 'new' librarians, i.e., those who in the 1870s had created a profession for themselves were being forced to accept and some were even leading the introduction of these strangers into their libraries.

In the 1970s, we are coming to terms with the greatly accelerated development of micro-reproduced materials and computerised compilations of dates. For both staff and users of libraries, the word library has perhaps obscured in the past the realization that the stock-in-trade of a library is the contents of the packages of the shelves as much as, and sometimes more than, the packages themselves. Few Librarians and other information workers, nowadays, make this mistake and most of them take a great deal of trouble to try to ensure that their clients customers users get the sort of information which they want in whatever medium it may be presented. This is a good point at which to say what is meant by information. Anything contains information and information may relate to anything. It has to be sought and worked upon to be any use to anyone. It is passive until someone acts upon it early rock books, clay books and books of many other kinds to the present day conceivable forms of presenting knowledge in a 'readable' form runs the story of the evolution and development of libraries.

Over the years various writers have prophesied the death of the book some have seen the cause of that death as competition from new media while others have predicted that political regime unsympathetic to free exchange of information would prefer more controllable means of communication. In spite of such forecasts, the book constitutes the commonest and most popular type of stock in most types of library today.

Growth and Development of Libraries in India

The whole story of development of the libraries in India can it studied under three distinct headings—

— the libraries of ancient India
— the libraries in medieval India and
— the libraries of modern India

1. Libraries of Ancient India

In ancient times, the hand written books or the manuscripts were the only source of recording the information for future use and they are supposed to comprise the library at the time. Our living testimony of the Vedas, the Upanishads and the epics and the Buddhist religious literature indicates, that even at an early date progress in the art of writing was appreciated. Jainism and Buddhism laid emphasis upon the systems of organized brotherhood accommodated in rock-cut halls, *Viharas* or monasteries. The Brahmanical systems also followed suit with similar institutions like *Mathas* and regular colleges.

The availability of written material from the 4th century B.C points out to the definite existence of places for "Storing" and making manuscripts accessible to the class. The Buddhist system of education and learning indicates the essential requirement of libraries. The Buddhist *Viharas* at Nalanda, Odantapuri and other similar centres were de facto universities in those days and each one of them possessed adequate library facilities. The accounts of Fa-hien, Hiuen-tsang and I-tsing, bring the first hand evidences can be considered as authentic and original in this regard.

A change reflecting the impact of literary activities on the growth and development of libraries came around the Gupta period (A.D. 320-615) when in the wake of the Hindu-Renaissance, the provision of library facilities was officially encouraged. The library, in the Gupta's period, was well planned and it seems to have housed both the Buddhist and the non-Buddhist literature.

The Nalanda University, seat of learning, around 400-450 AD was possessing the library situated in a special area known by the poetical name the *Dharmaganja* (Piety mart), which comprised three huge buildings, called the *Ratnasagara,* the *Ratnodadhi* and the *Ratnaranjaka,* of which the *Ratnasagara* was a nine-storeyed building and housed the collection of manuscripts and rare sacred works like "*Prajnaparamita sutra*" etc.

The university of Nalanda and its library flourished down to the 12th century A.D. until Bakhtiyar Khilji sacked it in 1197-1203 A.D.

The other world famous universities like *Vikramasila*, the *Vallabhi* and the *Kanchi* were coming up in other parts of the country during the period from the 5th century A.D. to the 8th century A.D. All these were having the rich libraries.

The university of Sompuri also had its own library. *Navadwipa* in the West Bengal, the last of the famous seats of learning in Eastern India reached its height of glory from A.D. 1063 to 1106 as a centre of intellectual excellence as well as its rich library facilities. However, this library, too was destroyed along with the centre by Bakhtiyar Khilji. The *Nagarjuna Vidyapeeth* was situated in South India at Amaravati, on the banks of the Krishan flourished about the 7th century A.D. Its library housed in the top floor of the five storeyed building of the university had an enormous collection on the Buddhist philosophy.

2. Libraries in Medieval India

The growth and development of libraries in medieval India presents an interesting historical scenario, in which we come across epochs of both high and low profiles of development form the times of destruction and disregard to the time of committed efforts for the development of libraries. Two factors, during this period, had a far reaching influence on the growth and development of libraries in India. One during the period from A.D. 800 to 1200, the northern and the southern halves of the subcontinent came into closer contact and, the other, the growing literary, scientific, religious and philosophical activities which were promoted more after the establishment of the Mughal Empire in India.

The name of Jalal-ud-din Khilji deserves special mention who himself being a poet remained surrounded by eminent men like Amir Khusrau, Tajdu-din Iraqu, Khwajah Amir Hasan Sijzi, Muyyid Diwanch, Amir Arslan Quali, and Baqui Khatir. He established the imperial library at Delhi and appointed Amir Khusrau as its librarian.

With the advent of the Mughals in India, libraries along with other institutions of social and cultural value received considerable impetus. One trait common to all of the Mughal empherors, from Babur to Aurangzeb, was that they all patronized learning and scholarship, and also maintained their palace libraries.

Babur was very fond of books and took keen interest in the development of his library. He regularly used his library which was in the Delhi Fort. In 1525, he took possession of the personal library of Ghazi Khan. During his reign he built libraries in "*Madrasa*".

Babur was succeeded by his elder son, Humayun, in 1530 A.D., who was also a scholar and a great lover of books. Even at the time of his expeditions to Bengal and Gujarat he carried his library with him. The emperor's promotion of the cause of libraries is further emphasized by the fact that he converted a pleasure-house in the Purana Qila of Delhi into a library.

Akbar the great (A.D. 1556-1605), succeeded Humayun. The growth and development of libraries in medieval India got much boosted during his reign. The imperial library's collection of books was enriched to a large extent, which came mostly from some of the private libraries and also from the libraries of Gujarat, Jaunpur, Kashmir, Bihar, Bengal and the Deccan. During the reign of Akbar, there functioned a regular translation bureau and many important volumes were added to the Imperial library. He was not satisfied with the collection development only. He also wanted to develop the art and science of librarianship, so he introduced science in management, classification and storage of books in his Imperial library. He also appointed Faizi, the great Persian scholar, as the Librarian of the Imperial library and Mulla Pir Muhammad that of his personal library. He created a separate department for the libraries to look after not only the state library, but also the public libraries located in the capital.

After the death of Akbar, an inventory of the Imperial properties housed in the fort of Agra. The Imperial library contained 24,000 illustrated and well bound volumes. The approximate price of the collection was Rs. 64,63,131.

Emperor Jahangir (A.D. 1605-1627) the successor of Akbar, ordered that the properties of rich heirless men should be utilized for building and repairing *Madrasas*, monasteries and libraries. He enriched the collection of Imperial library and added a picture Gallery to it. During his time, Maktab Khan was the superintendent of both the Imperial library and the Picture Gallery. In addition to the Imperial library, he also organized a personal library for his own use containing a number of books on various subjects.

In 1783 A.D., Nadir Shah in his invasion carried away with him the celebrated Imperial library. Thus, the imperial library of the Mughal emperors met an inglorious end.

Among the other contemporary libraries, the valuable collections of Maharaja Chikka Dev Raya (A.D. 1672-1740) of Mysore and Maharaja Sawai Jai Singh II (A.D. 1699-1743) of Jaipur deserve special mention.

The decline of the Mughal power over India from the 18th century onwards, paved the way for the spread of the British influence.

3. Libraries of Modern India

(a) 19th Century Libraries

The starting of the modern library movement can be seen in the first half of the 19th century. It was during that period that the public libraries were established with the support of the Europeans at Calcutta, Madras and Bombay. In this period, particularly in the context of academic libraries, the important events are (i) The Charter Act of 1813; (ii) The birth and progress of the Fort William College and the Serampore Colleges; (iii) Establishment of the calcutta, the Madras and the Bombay Universities, as per the famous despatch of Charles Wood (1854); and (iv) the Hunter Commission.

One direct result of the Charter Act of 1813 was the opening of a few colleges, such as, the C.M.S. College in Kottayam, the Hindu (Presidency) College in Calcutta in 1816, and the Raven Shaw College in Cuttak in 1816 with their own libraries the day they were established. The library at the Fort William had a well rounded collection in the Hindustani, the Persian, and the Arabic languages with emphasis on the collection of the Eastern manuscripts. With the establishment of the Calcutta University, on January 24, 1857, a new era of higher education and academic libraries started in India.

The foundation-stone for the Bombay University (1857) library was laid down, on March 1, 1869 due to the efforts of some businessmen. The university library was formally opened to the students, the faculty and the administrators on February 27, 1880.

Madras University founded in 1857 remained without a library for fifty years of its existence. It was only in 1907 that the Madras University was able to get its first university library through donations.

Besides, various public libraries were also established around this time. The Indore General Public Library was founded in 1854 by Maharaja Tukoji Rao Holkar II. He founded the present Indore General Library in the Huzuriya Mahal of the old palace and provided a donation of Rupees 500 and a recurring grant of Rupees 12 per month for it. This oldest and the premier public library known as the Kitab Ghar till 1866 had to pass through many vicissitudes during its chequered existence. After being shifted from the palace, the library was shifted to many places in the city till 1909, when it came to occupy the present building situated in the heart of the city the Rajwade Chowk.

The Connemara public library at Madras was founded in 1860, which was started as a small museum library owing to the efforts of one Captain Jesse Mitchel and was shifted to its present premises when Dr. Edgar Thurston was superintendent of the museum. Khuda Baksh Oriental Public library, at Patna was founded in 1879. The library owes its origin to Maulvi Muhammad Baksh Khan, who at the time of his death in July 1876 left a collection of 14,000 volumes, has one of the richest collections in the world of the ancient Persian and Arabic manuscripts and of the Chinese, the Central Asian, the Persian and the Indian paintings. The library was opened to public in 1891 and the government of Bengal was made its trustee. When Bihar was separated from Bengal, the Bihar government became its trustee. In 1962, the Government of India took over its management. In 1969, the Parliament passed the Khuda Baksh Library Act, declaring it as an institution of national importance and took the full financial and administrative responsibilities for it.

Another public library, the Adyar library in 1886 near Madras with the implicit goal of making it a temple of all faiths, was founded by Col. H.S. Olcott, the first president of the theosophical society, with a gift of his personal collection of about 200 books on a wide variety of subjects, relating to Indology, Indian Philosophy, mysticism and magic. The library was opened on December 28, 1886.

(b) Libraries onwards 1947

The year 1947 is significant not only from the point of view of India's political and economic growth, the assertion of her ethos and transformation to a new era of development but also for the growth and development of libraries in India, whether general or the specialized ones.

The first significant move in this direction being the change of the name of the Imperial library as the national library, by the Imperial Library, change of Name, Act, passed in 1948.

The Delhi library was established in 1951 by the Ministry of Education, Government of India, with financial and technical assistance from the UNESCO as a pilot project.

The library of the Lal Bhai Dalpat Bhai Institute of Indology, Ahmedabad has good collection of books on Indology. Another important instance of the growth of an Indological library is that of the Ananthachary Indological Research Institute at Bombay, which was founded on October 24, 1974. The Institute of Art and Culture at Calcutta, which was established in the year 1966 to preserve the artistic and cultural heritage of India, has an excellent collection on over three thousand books on world's art and culture. Another such institute is the Abul Kalam Azad Oriental Research Institute, which was founded in 1959 at Hyderabad. The Arabic and Persian Research Institute, Tonk (Rajasthan) is one of the prominent and premier institutes of India, forming an enviable national heritage. The library of this institute is very rich. The Raja Ram Mohan Roy library foundation was established in 1972. Various libraries in the field of social sciences and the sciences established after independence; to name fews are :

National Archives of India, Delhi (1947), National Institute of Mental Health and Neuro-sciences, Bangalore (1954), Small Industry Extension Training Institute, Hyderabad (1956), Directorate of Adult Education, Delhi (1956), International Institute for Population Studies, Bombay (1956), National Council of Applied Economic Research, New Delhi (1956), Institute of Economic Growth, Delhi (1958), Institute of Manpower Research, New Delhi (1960), Indian Institute of Management, Calcutta (1961), National Council of Educational Research and Training, New Delhi (1961), National Council of Educational Research and Training, New Delhi (1961), Indian Institute of Management, Ahmedabad (1962), Tribal Cultural Research and Training Institute, Hyderabad (1964), Institute of Research and Business Administration, Allahabad (1965), Indian Institute of Mass Communication, Delhi (1965), National Institute of Rural Development, Hyderabad (1965), Central Institute of Indian Languages, Mysore (1969), Indian Council of Social Science Research (ICSSR) New Delhi, in (1969), Centre for Decentralised Industries, Bombay (1970), Centre for Development Studies, Trivandrum (1970), National Institute of Planning and Administration, New Delhi (1971), Institute for Social and Economic Changes, Bangalore (1972), and Haeres Institute of

Indian History and Culture, Bombay (1976), in the field of social sciences.

The libraries of science field include INSDOC, CSIR, Vikram Sarabhi Space Centre, Central Fuel Research Institute, the Central Glass and Ceramic Research Institute, the National Metallurgical Laboratory, the Central Road Research Institute, the Central Building Research Institute, the National Aeronautical Laboratory, National Environmental Engineering Research Institute etc. These have good collections of specialized literature in specialized fields.

The seven IIT's established at Mumbai, Delhi, Kanpur, Gauhati, Kharagpur, Madras and Roorkee have good libraries.

In the public sector, Hindustan Aeronautics Ltd., the Hindustan Machine Tools Ltd., the Hindustan Steel Ltd., the Oil and Natural Gas Commission, the National Coal Development Corporation, the Steel Authority of India, Birla Group, the Larsen and Toubro etc. have their own libraries of scientific literature which meet requirements of their scientists.

Among others are, American Centre library, and the libraries of institutes like DRDO, DESIDOC, SENDOC, NISSAT, TERI, ICMR, NASSDOC etc. And recently with the establishment of INFLIBNET at Ahemdabad in 1988 and with its extending activities in the form of UGC-INFONET since 2004, the libraries are moving ahead. A forum or the consortium has been initiated the accessing e-books and the e-journals with this new initiative. The day is not more for when the people will really in position to a have the library use siting in their home or the office with out going actually to the libraries.

Q. : Discuss the role of libraries in the changing society.

or

Discuss in details the importance and need of libraries in modern society.

Ans. : The word library is derived from Latin word *Library* which itself came from word *Liber* meaning the bark. As in ancient times, the barks of the plants were used to write. Hence by suffixing word ary (of), the library word came into existence. In Hindi, the library is called as *Pustakalaya,* which is combination of two words *Pustak + Aalaya* meaning the house of books. Generally, in a library three things are seen :

(i) collection of books,

(ii) their use by readers, and

(iii) the staff

So library is called as trinity of these three things. Libraries have been defined variously as under :

Webester's 3rd New International Dictionary, 1961 edition, defines the library as 'A collection of books, manuscripts and other materials for study or reading, kept for convenient use or enjoyment. It is a room, a section or series of sections, of a building or a building itself given over to books, manuscripts, musical scores or other literary and sometimes artistic materials (e.g. painting or musical recordings) usually kept in some convenient order for use but not for sale.'

Gerald Johnson writes, "The quickest and the easiest access to the world's best thought is through public library". There is no gain saying the fact that a library houses the greatest thoughts of the world for, books-a constituent of the library - are said to be the greatest creation of the humans, who is the greatest creation of the God. Thus, the library a place where the greatest creation of the greatest creation is housed in an a organised way for the use of one and all.

Until recently the library was considered to be a "Store house for the recorded experience of mankind"or "a place set apart to contain books for reading, study or reference". The library was thus expected to collect, arrange and preserve reading material and makes these available on demand. A library that performed these four functions was supposed to have functioned satisfactorily. But the library of today not only opens its door more widely, but also has moved out of its four walls to reach larger target groups. Libraries of today are expected to do, and are doing much more than this and have assumed diverse dimensions.

The library of today is complex institution as far as its operations, objectives, management, services and sources of finance are concerned. "It is concerned with the refreshment of man's spirit by the provision of books for relaxation and pleasure with assistance to the students and with provision of up-to-date technical, scientific and sociological information." The changed character of public libraries and the wide range of activities, which these are performing today, have made the library a social and cultural center and a center for satisfying the educational, cultural and informational needs of the society.

Need and Importance of Libraries

The need and importance of the Libraries can be studied under following heads.

1. Library in Education : The education aims at (i) the imparting of knowledge (ii) the incalculation of values and (iii) the imparting of vocational skills.

There is both formal and non-formal education. Formal education is the one that an individual undergoes by enrolling himself in an educational institution like a school or a college or a university and through constant teacher student contacts. In non-formal deduction there is no such institutional base for education; one educate himself through correspondence courses or with the help private tuition or through own self-study.

Every institution of formal eduction, be it a school, college or university, should have a library attached to it. It should have a collection of books relevant to its courses of study. Students should be encouraged to read books and imbibe the knowledge contained in them. At the earlier stages of education like the school this should be done to supplement the class room teaching. At later stages, particularly in colleges and universities, the focal point of learning should gradually shift from the class room to the library. It is through the extensive reading of a variety of books bearing on a subject that a student will be able to acquire in-depth knowledge of the subject. By being able to analyse and compare different view points as expounded in different books, a student will be able to develop his capacity for analytical and critical thinking. This will enable him to formulate independent view points and opinions. The role of the library in fostering the intellectual development of the students cannot be over emphasized.

Apart from the school, college and university libraries, the public libraries too have a responsibility to support formal education. For this purpose, it must stock books of academic nature suitable for students and teachers of the educational institutions in its area and make the books available for them. It must be remembered in this context that a public library should serve every one in its community and it should not ignore the requirements of the teachers and students who form part of the community.

In non-formal education where the help of the teacher in minimal, it is the library that is the ministry. The students, by and large, have to acquire knowledge through self-study. Libraries of formal educational institutions as well as public libraries have a significant role to play in this aspect. The former should throw open their facilities to students of non-formal education in such a manner that the interests of their primary clientele are not adversely affected. Universities as the bodies that lay down academic standards and conduct examinations in the field of higher education have a special responsibility in this regard. They should try to make their library services reach as wide a clientele as possible including students of non-formal education. One way of making this possible is to establish branch libraries of the main university library at different places within its jurisdiction and making them accessible to the entire academic community in the area including students of non-formal education.

But the main responsibility of supporting non-formal education rests with the public library system. The library to which every one has access as a matter of right it the public library. A public library should try to discharge this responsibility by acquiring books and journals suited to the needs of the students of non-formal education in its area. The development of a sound public library system is an essential pre-requisite for the successful implementation of all non-formal education in its area. The development of a sound public library system is an essential pre-reqisite for the successful implementation of all non-formal educational programmes.

Besides, it is a special responsibility of the public library to work for the education of the illiterate people in its community through such media. It should also organize reading clubs and other programmes of oral communication for educating its illiterate clientele.

2. Library in Research : Supporting research is yet another important role of the library. Access to existing knowledge and information is essential for research. The knowledge that is newly created is primarily communicated through the media of journals, research reports and other similar publications. Every library attached to an institution engaged in research should have a strong collection of such publications to support research programmes. The libraries attached to universities, research organizations and research and development wing of industrial establishments play the key role in this respect.

3. Library in Cultural Activities : The cultural role of the library is that it preserves the cultural heritage of the human race as represented by the books. It should make available books which would bring to expression the creative talents of the individuals and develop their faculties for aesthetic appreciation. It should also organise cultural programmes like music concerts, dances, dramas, painting competitions for children, exhibition of paintings, etc. and thus enrich the cultural life of the community. These programmes primarily fall in the domain of public libraries.

4. Library in Disseminating Information : Libraries, are actually repositories of information and knowledge. Information is indispensable for any human activity aiming at social progress. The researcher, the teacher, the student, the administrator, the industrial and business manager, the artisan, the entrepreneur, the farmer, the worker in the factory and in the field, all need information to equip themselves better for the fruitful pursuit of their respective vocations. The basic information role of the library is to collect the materials containing the information required by the various sections of the society and disseminate the information to them through appropriate methods. It is primarily in this sense that a library is described as an information centre.

But a library has also an information role in the sense of providing information relating to the socio-economic needs of the people. A library can stock career information books and help those who are on the look out for choosing a career. Similarly well produced" how-to-do-it type of books" would be helpful in providing guidance to the youngsters in the society wanting to start some enterprise. In short, a library should be so equipped and organized that it will be able to serve its community with all types of information that may be in actual or potential demand

5. Library in spiritual and Ideological Realms : The books can be broadly divided into three categories– books of information, books of recreation and books of inspiration. Spiritual and religious books, books that propound ideological themes and other books of permanent value which may be described as classics are books of inspiration. They meet the spiritual, religious and ideological needs of their readers. Every library should have a representative collection of books of this type to inspire people to high ideals in life and inculcate values in them.

6. Library in Recreation : Healthy use of leisure is a matter of great importance in community life so that the leisure time is not devoted to negative and destructive activities. The library should cater to the recreational needs of its users by stocking books suited for the purpose. Novels and other forms of literature, works of art, books of travel, biographies, popular magazines, etc. are primarily books of recreation and they should have a place in every library. Besides, libraries, especially public libraries, should organise programmes of healthy recreation and entertainment like the performing arts, musical concerts, etc.

Library's Role in Changing Society

Human society has travelled a long journey from Stone Age to the Age of Technology. The age of technology, in which we are living today and the technological revolutions are founded on the pillars of information. Our present society is thus information-based society. The changes that are occurring in the multifarious facets of human life in modern society can be seen in the following:

— Social – population pressure, increasing urbanization, emphasis on rural development, mobility of population, group dynamics and pressures, etc;

— Economic – occupational patterns, income, prices, value, inflation, growth dynamics, economic developments at macro and micro-level, etc.;

— Political – political structures and systems, activities of political parties, legislatures and members in parliament as well as state assemblies, power structure, etc.;

— Educational – learning and teaching at all levels-formal and non-formal, learning and teaching materials, educational technology, etc,;

— Research and development – scientific, technological, social sciences, leading to knowledge creation, innovation, diffusion, dissemination, distribution and use, transfer of technology, etc,;

— Industry and business – production and distribution, technology acquisition, assessment and application, marketing and sales, etc.;

— Trade and commerce – import and export, international trade and commerce, etc.;

— Government and administration – planning, policy making, execution and management etc.;

— Cultural – fine arts and music, show business and entertainment, cinema, broadcasting TV etc.

The above facets of modern human life merely illustrate some of the more conspicuous factors of contemporary human life in which rapid changes are presently taking place.

These factors have radically changed the conventional function of the library. The flood of information has therefore to be controlled , analysed, and channeled so as to derive maximum benefit. This implies, taking steps to ensure that the available information reaches the right user. And there can possibly be no better institution than a library for collecting, storing, and disseminating right information to the needy user on one hand, and to find and locate right user for right information on the other hand. Libraries are thus indispensable for the society for meeting its informational needs. Interestingly alongside the library, new types of institutions like documentation centres, information analysis centres, data banks, resource centres, multimedia centres, etc. have sprung up in the last 30 years. Many of these developments have also provided new opportunities for commercialization of information products and services, thus paving the way for an information industry which is presently flourishing steadily. These rapid changing roles of the library has made an eminent information scientist to remark that "in a metaphorical sense, we are moving from a Ptolemaic world with the library at the centre to a Coperniean one with information at the centre and the library as one of its planets." This vividly brings out the changing dimensions of knowledge and information and the institutional mechanism to handle them.

Libraries are therefore indispensable for the society. These educate, inform and convert an individual into a better citizen. There is no gain saying the fact that the men and women who move and lead the world in any field are informed people. It makes information available in a better, organized and more economical manner to all its members. The opening of more and more libraries may reduce the number of prisons, police stations and courts of law. These institutions will also be needed in all times but in a library oriented society, their number would certainly be reduced.

2
Types of Libraries and Their Functions

Q. : What are the different types of libraries? Differentiate between academic library and the public library or a special library.

or

What is the difference between an academic library and a public library? Describe academic library in brief.

or

How a special library is different from an academic library and the public library?

Ans. : Libraries may broadly be categorized in following three types:

1. Public libraries
2. Academic libraries
3. Special libraries

1. PUBLIC LIBRARIES

Public library has been construed differently by different experts depending upon the importance they give to its objectives. It was a people's university for those who laid stress on educative aspect; it was a common man's cultural centre for those who had in mind its recreational role; for some it was a centre to provide authentic information in various aspects of life.

It is understood that a library which is open for every one, irrespective of age, sex, occupation, affiliation and social or economic status is a public library.

However, the most widely accepted definition of a public library was formulated by UNESCO in 1949 which was later revised in 1972 in what has come to known as the UNESCO Public Library Manifesto. The definition of a public library according to this manifesto is as follows:

It is a library which :

(i) is financed for the most part out of public funds;

(ii) charges no fees from readers and yet is open for full use by the public without distinction of caste creed or sex;

(iii) is intended as an auxiliary educational institution providing a means of self-education which is endless;

(iv) houses educative and informative materials giving reliable information freely and without partiality or prejudice on as wide a variety of subject as will satisfy the interest of readers.

UNESCO emphasis that a public library is that library which is opened by the state with legislative support, maintained out of public fund, and the services of which are available to all free of charge. Free public libraries were started in UK and USA much earlier.

Most of the libraries in our country would not fulfil all the conditions laid down by UNESCO. But still we have libraries with legislative support *i.e.*, established under the clear mandate of law. Such libraries are functioning in the eleven states, which have adopted library legislation. In other states, though libraries have not been established with legislative support, but these states also have government libraries, which are maintained out of public money.

Broadly speaking we have two types of public libraries in our country (i) Government public libraries, and (ii) non-government public libraries. Government libraries, though may not be essentially established under the mandate of law but are run by the state out of public fund and are more or less free libraries. Some of these may be charging a nominal amount as membership fee or deposit money for borrowing material for home reading. But consulting reading material in the library is normally free of charge in these libraries. Libraries run by local bodies such as municipality etc. may also be considered as government libraries because these are also maintained out of public money. Non-government libraries are run by variety of organization, trusts, institutions etc. Among these a few are aided (*i.e.*, receiving some aid or assistance from the government) and some are non-aided. To run their services these libraries normally charge some nominal amount from members, but consulting reading material (*i.e.*, books, newspapers, magazines etc.) inside the library is free in most of these libraries. We may therefore define a public library, in Indian context, as library thrown open to the public free of charge or on a nominal charge for some specific service.

Functions of a Public Library

A public library generally performs the following functions :

— It provides free and direct access to tools of information and education.

— It serves as an instrument of informal self-education.

— It acts as a centre for cultural and social activities of the local community.

— It stimulates thought and develop understanding among people and to strengthen the spirit of democracy, and

— It preserves the materials of local/regional cultural heritage.

Important functions of a public library may be presented under two broad headings, (i) Collection related functions, and (ii) Service related functions as under :

Collection Related Functions : The public library acquires, collects, organizes, and make available for use audiovisual materials to the public with an aim to:

(i) providing to the public, facilities for informal and life long self-education.

(ii) providing to them facilities to support their formal education by collecting books and other documents on various subjects and courses.

(iii) providing healthy literature for recreation and constructive use of leisure time.

(iv) meeting information need of the community.

(v) providing documents to support the civic and cultural engagements of the people; and

(vi) reach those who do not or can not reach it.

Service Related Functions : The public library performs wider range of functions and activities in order to serve the community more effectively. Some of such service-functions are :

(i) to provide guidance to its readers in locating and using the document of their interest.

(ii) to promote the use of the library by inviting people, publicizing the library's services and reaching the people at their door-steps. The tendency to serve only those who come or approach, results in a passive library. An active library reaches even those who do not or can not come to it; and

(iii) to serve as a social, cultural and intellectual power house for the community and for this purpose to employ efficient way of information retrieval, to organize extension activities, such as discussion on the current problems of the community, religious discourses after library hours and local festivals, book exhibition etc.

2. ACADEMIC LIBRARIES

An academic library is a library attached to an academic institution i.e., an institution engaged in teaching and/or research and imparting formal education to students who aspire to complete a particular course under a prescribed syllabus. Schools, colleges, universities and technological/engineering/medical institutions are some of such institutions. Thus there are various types of academic institutions which may vary from one another in respect of courses offered by these. Since academic libraries exist to cater the needs and requirements of their parent academic institution, these vary in shape, size, collection and services, depending upon the nature of the parent institution. For example, libraries attached to a school, college and even to an undergraduate college, a post graduate college, a medical college, an engineering college would be different from the rest in respect of collection, shape, size and services.

The following diagram broadly indicates the various types of libraries attached to the different educational institutions designed and developed in India:

Academic Libraries

- School
  - Primary
  - Middle
  - Secondary
  - Higher Secondary
- College
  - Polytechnics
  - Undergraduate
  - Postgraduate
  - Professional
- University
  - Conventional universities
  - Institutes of Science and Technology
  - Indian Institutes of Technology
  - Agriculture Universities
  - Indian Institutes of Management
  - Universities for Distance education and others

However, all academic libraries have common qualities in many respects. It is because all academic libraries exist to support the teaching and research programmes of their parent institutions. Besides having a good collection of reference books on variety of subjects, these emphasize on building up a strong collection concerning the courses offered by the institution.

(i) School Libraries

The broad ideals of the school education are:

— to prepare children and young students to acquire skills in the learning process; obtain a basic knowledge of one or more languages and a set core of subject, with specialisation in the last four years of school education. These preparations provide them a good foundation for going in for higher studies after the successful completion of the school programme or branch off for professional education or vocational training;

— to enable the children and young students to get an idea of the society in which they live and the surroundings in which they function and operate;

— to inculcate in young children and young students ethical values and build character so as to mould them into good citizens to play a positive role in the progress and development of the nation.

Thus, the libraries in the schools are established to serve these purposes. The objectives of school library may be :

— to procure, process and provide all documents as well as non-documents that can be the source of learning. Documents are in the form of books, magazines, dictionary, encyclopedia, directory etc. Non-documents are photographs, charts, globes, films, filmstrips, videotapes, audiocassettes, transparencies, slides, computer floppies, CD-ROMs, multi-media discs, etc.

— to process all the documents and non-documents in the systematic way of library classification and cataloguing, so that any student or teacher can use the in a friendly manner.
— to provide the support and guide the students in finding the source of information they are looking for.
— to develop a habit in the students to use the library more and more for their knowledge, educational developments and better future prospects.
— to support in the activities of school programme.
— to facilitate the need of teachers and students for the community development in the society.
— to act as a resource centre.
— to provide informal education.

Functions of School Library

The functions of a school library may be :

— Helps in self learning
— Information and Communication
— Self motivating environment
— Proper handling of library materials
— Morel education
— Education and training
— Professional developments in teachers
— Proper utilization of leisure
— Future developments
— Personality developments

(ii) Secondary School Libraries

If primary school libraries are designed to function and operate as integral parts of the educational programme at that state, the secondary school libraries maintain their separate identity, fulfilling all the requirements of the young students for learning and the teachers for teaching. Secondary school libraries support school programmes at three stages, viz. middle-classes 6 to 8, secondary-classes 9 and 10, and higher secondary-classes 11 and 12, constituting a total period of seven years of the school programme. These are crucial formative years of the children and good habits formed at this stage would be everlasting. So, the library has a very positive role to play and aim to achieve the following:

— inculcating the habit of using the school library, not only with reference to their reading for course requirements but also for reading for pleasure, general knowledge and recreation;

— development of skills for collecting information on any topic by consulting reference books;

— provide opportunities to visit other academic, special and public libraries to make the children get an idea of the library system in the country and use them at later stages of their lives.

Functions of Secondary School Libraries

The primary responsibility of the secondary school library is to build up a stock of books and kindred material reveal to the learning and teaching needs of the students and teachers respectively. The collection should adequately represent.

(i) an excellent stock of text books, both prescribed and others, (in multiple copies, if necessary) on all subjects related to courses of studies;

(ii) relatively more advanced books on all subjects for brighter students and teachers;

(iii) general books on popular science, biographies of great persons, travelogues, geographical explorations, sports and games and others that would create interest in reading;

(iv) Books of fiction, collection of short stories and other light reading materials;

(v) carefully assorted reference.

A secondary school library should offer the following services;

(i) Lending

(ii) Information and Reference Service

(iii) Guidance and advice

(iv) Preparation of reading list, in anticipation or response, on any topic,

(v) Current awareness service on current events, activities, personalities scientific and technological achievements, anything of national importance and international events of significance.

(vi) Other services for spreading the message of books and libraries, such as organization of book exhibitions of appropriate occasions organizing book talks by those who can hold the interest of students, e.g., competitions — oratorical contents, debates on current issue, essay writing, quiz programmes, etc.

(vii) Other routing services like display of jackets of currently acquired books, newspaper clippings, particularly those that are of interest to students, pictures and photographs of current events and activities and persons of importance.

Lending services enable students and teachers to borrow books and other materials according to a set of rules and regulations, for reading at home at their own study or leisure time and at their own pace. Students should be encouraged to make use of this facility.

(iii) College Libraries

College education provides a totally different environment for boys and girls who go for higher studies. Usually the classes comprise a large number of students and unlike school education, the students of college get much less individual attention from the teachers. The students, therefore, have to depend much more on themselves. Therefore, the college library is the automatic choice for the students to supplement their class room teaching.

Among the several objects and functions of the college, the following deserve special mention:

(i) Giving young men and women a wider and deeper understanding of the various disciplines;

(ii) Preparing the more precocious students for advanced studies in various disciplines;

(iii) Preparation of young men and women for shouldering the higher responsibilities of manning schools, government departments, civic organizations, commercial establishments, business and industry etc.;

(iv) Training young persons for various professions like law, medicine, engineering and technology;

(v) Training a body of more enlightened, knowledgeable and responsible citizenry.

In the translation into practice of all these objectives and functions, the college library has a central role to play.

Functions and Activities of a College Library

Generally, in order to satisfy the varied academic and extra curricular needs of both students and the teachers, a college library should acquire a wide variety of learning and teaching materials. These may be broadly grouped as below :

— A good collection of multiple copies of text books and other recommended books, at the rate of one copy for every ten users;

— Books of a more advanced nature for the benefit of the teachers and also for the use of the more precocious students;

— A wide range of reference books such as general and subject encyclopaedias, language and subject dictionaries, handbooks, yearbooks, manuals, biographical and geographical tools, biographies, fiction etc;

— A browsing collection of light reading material like travelogues, huinour books, art books, biographies, fiction etc;

— A select list of learned journals as well as popular ones, including back volumes;

— Audio-visual learning and teaching kits to include films, film strips, pictures, audio cassettes and discs, tape-slide kits, video-cassettes, etc.;

— Computer-aided teaching and learning material.

The most common services that are provided in college libraries are:

(i) Text book service

(ii) Lending

(iii) Reading Room

(iv) Reference

(v) Display of current additions or production of lists of current accessions;

(vi) Documentation services, only on specific request, to include:

Current awareness to literature, specially journals. Preparation of current lists of references Indexing/Abstracting services on projects and similar others;

(vii) Reprographic services

(viii) Audio visual services such as film shows, tape-slide demonstrations, computer-aided programmes etc.

(ix) Exhibitions and special display

(x) Assistance in the use of the library

The provision of lending in college libraries must stimulate active use of the collection. Borrowing privileges must be liberal and the lending procedures must be simple. The library should also endeavour to extend interlibrary loan facilities for materials which are not available in the college library.

The students should be given ready assistance in locating materials in the library, searching the library catalogue for specific items of information on documents available in the library, in methods of using indexing and abstracting services and locating factual information from reference tools.

The library should bring to the notice of the students and teachers, currently acquired materials through appropriate publications.

A special emphasis must be given to text book service. This not only meets the difficulties of economically poor students but makes a very positive contribution to the students.

(iv) University Libraries

The universities are the centres of higher education and research work. The objects and functions of a university may broadly be grouped as follows:

— to provide intellectual and managerial leadership to various fields of government, industry, health, engineering, law, defence, education, agriculture, etc. and imbue them with a sense of social purpose;

— to train a band of research workers in all the areas mentioned above so that the results of research could be harnessed to improve the quality of life of the people;

— to conserve knowledge and ideas for posterity;

— to foster the ideals of social justice, religious tolerance, national integration among its diverse people.

A university library is a library attached to a university, which exists to cater to the needs and requirements of students and teachers and to support the teaching and research programmes of the university. So, the library documentation and information services in a university library have also to be highly organized with considerable professional expertize and knowledge of subjects.

During the past, university education was based on dictation: teachers used to dictate and students used to listen to or note. Later, the need and importance of libraries in an university has been realised and accepted by many authorities. For example, the Kothari Commission recognizes the library as the heart of the university. Similarly, the UGC (UK) report maintained some seventy years ago, "The character and efficiency of a university may be gauged by its treatment of its central organ, the library." The report stresses, "An adequate library is not only the basis of all teachings and study: it is an essential condition of research without which addition can not be made to the sum of human knowledge." An eminent educationist Cyril Norwood in his speech at the Annual Conference of ASLIB (1936) said firmly, "it is a better proof of education to know how to use a library than to possess a university degree." It is therefore an accepted fact that libraries are of paramount importance for universities. Someone has rightly said, "There are three distinguishing marks of a university - a group of students, a corps of instructors, and collection of books and of these the most important is collection of books."

Functions of University Libraries

University libraries support and help the university in achieving the objectives of the university. In short, the functions which a university library is expected to perform may be enumerated as under :

(i) to acquire, process, organize and make available reading and other materials to students, teachers and other members of the university so as to enable them to complete their reading, teaching, research, and other assignments.

(ii) In addition to the above the university library is also expected to provide material to its users for (i) arousing their intellectual curiosity and sharpening intellectual faculty; (ii) stimulating imagination, reasoning and critical faculty, (iii) refining their ethical and cultural values (iv) making them aware of their environment and development around them (v) informing and guiding them with regard to their further education, profession or occupation.

(iii) To encourage the use of library by (i) initiating the fresh students and teachers, (ii) taking up readers education programmes *i.e.*, imparting instructions in the use of the library and issuing brochures etc. for this purpose.

(iv) Current Awareness services including (a) Current contents of journals; (b) Alerting services to important literature in select fields; (c) Selective Dissemination of information; (d) Newspaper clipping service; and Condensation services like, (a) Preparation of abstracts in specific topics (b) Digest services ; (c) Preparation of reviews/progress/advances on specific subjects; (d) State-of-Art-reports is also expected to be served for the readers.

(v) To adopt new technology e.g. computerization in certain areas with a view to provide purposeful service in minimum possible time.

Other functions may include :

(i) Document supply services

(ii) Reprographics services

(iii) Translation services etc.

3. SPECIAL LIBRARIES

A special library is one which serves a particular group of people, such as the employees of a firm or government department, or the staff and members of a professional or research organization. Such a library deals essentially in information. It is not true, as some writers suggest, that books do not matter in a special library; it is true that they may be less important than material like research reports, pamphlets, periodical articles, news-cuttings, trade-literature and even letters, which may be regarded as 'ephemeral' in the public or academic library.

The essential purpose of the special library is to provide information which will assist its parent organization. To do this adequately the library should hold a reasonably high position in the organization structure, so that it knows the organisations's policies and interests.

Special libraries are formed in research and development

establishments, government departments, directorates, bureaus, industrial and business undertakings, learned societies and professional associations, trade and business associations, hospitals and health services, social and welfare organisations, museums, national gallery of arts, etc. However special libraries are established to serve a particular group of users or an activity or specialists working on a subject or a group of subjects or a particular type of documents, etc. The following table illustrates these units:

Distinguishing Aspects	**Special Library**
Special user groups	Libraries for the Blind; Children; Hospital patients
Kind of activity	Nutrition (the Library of the National Institute of Nutrition, Hyderabad)
Specialising in a group of subjects	Food Science and Technology (the Library of the Central Food and Technological Research Institute, Mysore)
Type of documents	A film library; a video cassette library; a manuscript library.

Functions and Features of Special Libraries

The main features of a special library may be pointed out as under:

(i) It lays marked emphasis on special collection, i.e., collection in some specific field. The collection is build up keeping in view the objectives and policies of parent organization. The collection may also fulfil research requirements of the organization but does not aim at collecting documents relating to formal education.

(ii) It has specialist clientele with common interest *i.e.*, all the clientele's interest and requirements revolve round achieving the objectives and goals set by the organization under clearly spelt policy statements. The clientele normally have no individual interests or requirements, or at least, the library is not set up with this objectives.

(iii) It requires highly skilled and professionally competent staff and advanced mechanical and electronic equipments so as to provide the desired service in the quickest possible time.

(iv) *Interest of Parent Ogranization* : For special library the interest of the parent organisation is more important than the interest of an individual, if any. Other types of libraries are also supposed to care for the objectives and policies of the parent organization, but at the same time these give due weightage to the individual requirements of the clientele. This is more true in case of a public library.

(v) Besides, a wide variety of reader's services is given by the special libraries to its readers. These include:

(a) *Reference Services* : Reference and research services range from answering simple reference questions to undertaking complex research and literature services. Users are usually assisted in the pursuit of their own search for literature but quite often information expertize is made available in locating requested information and transmitting them in the most useful form. In fact, expertise is built into the special libraries staff to handle complicated and complex problems of information handling. Some special libraries offer translation service either providing in-house service or obtaining them from outside sources. In most of the special libraries, a close working relationship exists between the library staff and users to derive the maximum benefit from the library units.

(b) *Current Awareness Service* : Special libraries have developed a wide range of services to keep their users informed of new and current developments. Routing of current issues of periodicals is one of the most common functions of special libraries. The library periodically surveys its clientele as to which periodicals they wish to see on a regular basis, then circulates them to readers, as issues arrive. Current acquisition bulletins, index to current periodicals and title alerts are some of the different types of current awareness services provided by special libraries.

(c) *Anticipatory Service* : Besides these services, annotated lists, abstract bulletins, news summaries, digests or other types of anticipatory service are also provided by special libraries. In recent decades, many of the special libraries provide computer based selective dissemination of information (SDI) service. In India, SDI services are also provided but not necessarily through computers.

(d) *Retrieval Services* : Abstracting, indexing and preparation of digests are of paramount importance in special libraries. Special project and retrospective files are built up in special libraries for meeting their requirements on projects or requirements for new product or process development.

3
Five Laws of Library Science

Q. : Write an essay on the five laws of library science.

or

What are the five laws of library science? Discuss their implications on library authority, books, readers and the staff.

or

Books are for use. Discuss this law.

or

What are the five laws of library science? Discuss first law of library science in detail.

or

Discuss the implication of the fifth of library science for the library work.

or

What are the five laws of library science? Library science is a growing organism, discuss this law in detail.

Ans. : A library is a place where books are collected, they are organized so that the information contained in them is disseminated to the desired points. In order to let the library serve its purpose, Dr. Ranganathan, the then Librarian of the University of Madras, enuciated the *Five laws of Library science* in 1928. These principles could tell us what should be done in the library field to make library organization, management and operation efficient and to universalize its services. These basic principles may also contain in a latent form many other practices not known now and may bring them to surface as the boundary conditions set by the society change. Every activity relating to a library has a rational in one or another of these laws or in all of them collectively. The Laws are:

— Books Are For Use

— Every Reader His/Her Book

— Every Books Its Reader

— Save the Time of the Reader

— Library is a Growing Organism

1. Books are for use

This is the first law of library science, which messages that the books are meant for use and they should be freely used. The first and the foremost duty of the librarian is to ensure proper use of books available in the library. He can ensure the maximum use of books by taking in account the following factors:

(i) Location : The location of a library is an important factor for this law to be fulfilled. There are two different views regarding the location of a library. One view suggests that a remote area is the most suitable place for a library. The supporters of this view say that a calm, quiet and distantly located place is the right place for a library. They are of the opinion that a library is a place for serious study, a lonely place which is far from the crowds is suitable for it. So the selected few will come to study and not all.

The second view is that a library should be situated at a central place. A school library should be located at a prominent place in the school where the students may take easy notice of it. So too a college library. The description of a university library as the heart of the university should be reflected in its geographical location also. The point to be kept in view is the easy accessibility of the library to its users.

(ii) Open Access : The Librarian should adopt the open access system in the library. In this system, every reader is allowed to go to shelves and choose the books of his interest. If saves the time because a reader does not have to wait for the library staff to trace the desired book of his interest. In case, he does not find the desired book on the shelves, he can choose some other books to substitute the book which he was looking for. Hence open access enhances the use of books.

(iii) Library Hours : The first law demands that the library should be kept open during the hours which are most suitable to the readers.

Many libraries in our country do not pay attention to this message. School libraries, college libraries and public libraries are particularly careless in this matter as many of them are kept open when their clientele are engaged otherwise and are not able to visit the library. Take the example of a public library, it must function in the evening so that people engaged in various jobs and professions and students can use it after finishing their regular work. Similarly an academic library should be kept open beyond the normal hours also when the students are free from the class rooms. Hence the opening of the library for late hours will increase the use of books in the library.

(iv) Library Building and Furniture : In order to promote the use of books, the library must have a functional library building and at the same time it should be aesthetic. If the racks in which the books are kept, are too tall and to the books on the top shelves cannot be easily reached, the use of books becomes difficult. The furniture used in children libraries should be specially designed keeping in view the goal of the promotion of the use of books. The furniture should also be attractive and comfortable so that users will feel tempted to frequent the library.

(v) Library Staff : The exception of the first law is that the library staff should be attentive, cheerful and carers for books and readers. They should possess the qualifications that would enable them to organize the library efficiently and provide satisfactory services. This would ensure the proper use of books. But more important than formal qualifications, are perhaps the personal qualities of the library staff. The staff should render helping hand to the readers. They should not be considered as nuisance but as customers. There are different sort of readers, some may be shy, and owing to shy nature or complexity of library techniques, they may not find the desired books. The library staff therefore, should take keen interests in knowing the needs and requirements. The staff should always remember that everything that they do in the library is a means towards an end and the end is service to readers. If a potential library user encounters an unhelpful attitude on the part of any member of the staff, he is sure to turn away permanently from the library. The result is that the cause of the first law is not served. The credibility of the staff, both in respect of their knowledgeability and their personal attitude to readers, is a crucial factor in the promotion of the use of books.

2. Every Reader His/Her Book

This is the second law of library science. The first law revolts against the concept of "Books are for preservation" and "replaces books are for use." This law stands for the mandatory provision of library service to each according to his need. Every reader of a library should have the books he wants. It advocates the universalization and democratization of library service. In the earlier days, only a privileged few belonging to the aristocracy and the upper classes of the society were given access to libraries and books and the masses were kept out. But with the advent of democracy which ensured participation of every citizen in governance, the position drastically changed. Democracy, for its sustenance and survival, needed an educated, knowledgeable and responsible citizenry. So, education and the acquisition of knowledge through whatever institution this was possible, became a societal imperative. Thus the 2nd law fixes some responsibilities on the state, the library authority, library staff and the readers. These are discussed as below :

(i) Obligation of the State : It is the obligation of the state to develop and maintain a library system that is capable of providing adequate library service to all the people. This is preferably done through legislation which should make provision for the financial support of the library system and the coordination of the activities of its different units. A prior goal should be set for the type of library system and services best suited for a society and the legislation should be so framed that it would serve as an effective means for achieving the goal. Dr. Ranganathan has discussed the obligation of the state under three heads:

(a) Finance (b) Legislation (c) Coordination

(a) Finance : Adequate finance is the first requirement for running a library or a chain of the libraries to serve the need for all. The state may provide finance in two ways, firstly by sanctioning a grant and secondly by levying library cess. In the first method, the state may allocate a fixed amount of money per year or during a plan period for library development. In the second method, the state authorities and the local authority to levy library cess as surcharge on certain taxes such as property tax etc. The state normally contributes equal or more amount. These two methods are means to provide finance for running public library service in particular states. In short, the 2nd law insists that the state should make provision for sufficient finance for running library services in the country.

(b) Library Legislation : India is one of the democratic countries. Every citizen has the right to read and right to access to reading materials. The state may therefore make available them facilities for reading throughout their life. This is the demand of second law. This can be achieved by enacting library legislation in the states. Many countries have library legislation years back but India is lagging behind. After the independence many states enacted library legislation still there some states where legislation has not been enacted. Thus, second law lays emphasis that the states should consider library legislation with a view to providing every reader his/her book.

(c) Coordination : The coordination implies coordinating and linking library service at each level. It is found that all the libraries or the most libraries are functioning in isolation. It is therefore essential to coordinate libraries and their service at each level according to the spirit of the second law. Coordination ensures maximum utilization of the available resources of a country or state. In such a system all libraries right from the national library to state library, district libraries, book libraries and village libraries and they are linked with each other in the form of chain. Book collection and services of one library are made available to other libraries when needed.

(ii) Obligation of the Library Authority : As far as the Library Authority is concerned, its obligation necessitated by the Second Law is in respect of (a) choice of books and (b) choice of staff.

(a) Choice of books : No library has ever enough funds to buy all the books that it needs. Hence to provide every reader his book, the second law requires the librarians to know the subjects standards and the languages of the books used. It indicates that a library should select books on all the major occupations of its actual and potential readers. In fact, systematic user surveys are conducted in modern libraries to ascertain the book requirements of their clientele in order to frame their policy of selection and acquisition. User surveys are important to determine user requirements for books, to build up a collection in a library. To buy a book that has no actual or potential demand in preference to a book that is in demand is a violation of the second law.

(b) Choice of Staff : The second law desires an adequate library staff. Any library authority should realize the need for an adequate devoted staff to show every reader how to use books as tools and libraries as workshops. This highlights the duty of library staff.

Frequently, a library finds itself in such a predicament for want of adequate and competent staff. The second law dictates that this should not happen and that the Library Authority should not grudge the provision of staff which would obviate such situations.

(iii) Obligation of the staff : But it is not enough if the Library Authority makes adequate and competent staff available. They have to be constantly conscious of the second law in their work and conduct and be guided by its message.

The second law demands an earnest staff with a sense of duty to carry out the message. The business of the librarians in not only the provision for every reader with his/her book but also to know the reader to know the documents and activity help every reader to find his/her book. This phase of work is known as reference service. The role of the reference librarian is like that of an advisor. He is a companion, who is more familiar with character of the documents. He should have intimate knowledge of Bibliographies and Indexing and Abstracting services available in particular subjects. From the side of readers too, the request for such pin pointed service should come without any hesitation.

Sometimes matter of interest to a reader may be contained in a chapter or a few pages of a book. He may not consider the book as of interest to him and amy not look it up in the normal course. Therefore there is every chance of the reader missing such matter and the second law would feel aggrieved. To avoid such a contingency, the library catalogue should have profuse subject analytical or cross reference entries which would draw the attention of readers to the contents of books in which they are interested.

(iv) Obligation of the Reader : The reader also has certain responsibilities cast on him by the second law. It particularly wants him to observe the library rules in respect of the duration of the loan of book. If a reader retains a book beyond the period of loan, he is depriving other readers who may want to use the books. There are readers who misplace books with a view to monopolies their use, tear of pages from books and even steal books. The result is a gross violation of the second law. The readers should be made conscious of the consequences of such acts through a programme of instruction in library use or User Education programs in libraries.

Adoption of the above principle in the organization of the libraries will extend the scope of use of documents to each and all. If every member of the community has the privilege of using the material in library, the responsibility of the library for providing adequate material of all types increases. The reader should behave in the library in a manner they expect others to behave. This is the message of the 2nd law "Every reader his/her book".

3. Every Books Its Reader

Third law of library science is Every Book its Reader. The impact of the third law is that the library authority and the library staff should adopt such methods and techniques that will ensure that every book or reading material which is in the library finds its reader. The most effective way of satisfying the Third Law is to introduce an arrangement in which the books have a chance of catching the attention of readers. This is possible in the Open Access System. In this system, books are arranged in open shelves in the classified order and readers have freedom of access to them. In the course of the readers' browsing through the shelves, they may come across some books of interest to them the existence of which they were not aware of. Thus, the chances of readers noticing the books and reading them are enhanced in the open access system.

The advantages of open access to library shelves provide an opportunity to users to get access to other books in the library kept along with the particular book in which the user may be interested. In this process of browsing, he gets not only more information about the books in his field of interest, but also in related fields. This opportunity of browsing is not available to a user in a closed access library.

The disadvantages of open access are that books get quiet often misplaced on shelves by readers, which may obstruct other users in getting the benefit of browsing. Unsocial activities such as tearing pages from books, stealing, deliberate hiding of books may cause problems. Although this unsocial behaviour of some users can be controlled, they cannot be totally eliminated. However the advantages of open access, i.e., meeting a primary objective of library service, outweighs the disadvantages.

Dr. Ranganthan also said that loss of books in insignificant in view of greatly increased use of libraries. The benefit of open access is undisputable whereas the possible of books is small. Unfortunately the administration in many parts of the country not yet prepared to this logic and many a time, the librarian or the library staff has to suffer. Thus, the librarian is supposed to be the philosopher, the scientist and the scholar if the benefits of open access system are to be achieved.

Shelf arrangement, catalogue entries, entries, reference service, the opening of popular departments, publicity methods and the extension work etc. are the methods and devices that have been suggested by Dr. Ranganathan to fulfill the aims and objectives of the Third Law.

(i) Shelf Arrangement : To get full realization of the third law, open access system is not sufficient. It should be supplement with other devices, like shelf arrangement which is prerequisite for the success for this law. It demands that the books on the shelves of the library are arranged in such a helpful sequence that the reader is guided from one book to another automatically and from one shelf to another till he arrives at the desired book.

Dr. Ranganathan suggested that to attract the attention of the reader, the library staff should display the acquired "Recent additions" somewhere near the entrance of the library entrance. This is the shelf that attracts the readers. It will help in establishing fresh contact between the books and the readers. Arranging books on small shelves or showcases with captions "Book work looking", "Interesting Books", "Long forgotten but useful books" etc. will attract the attention of the reader. Thus, the will, throughout arrangement is necessary to find book its reader.

(ii) Catalogue : The catalogue can be of immense help in this matter. The main entries in the classified part reflect the arrangement on the shelves. Subject analytical and reference found in the classified part help in the hidden part of the books. The class index entries and book index entries help every book in getting its reader.

(iii) Reference Service : The open access system, a good arrangement on the shelves and subject analytical will not be adequate to find the book its reader, if there is no one in the library to interpret them to the readers. The books are silent, they cannot reach the hands of readers till their thought content is brought to the notice of the readers by the reference staff. Thus, the third law requires the provision of human beings as conversing agents for books. The reference staff must know the qualities of the books and other documents in the library. This direct contact with the readers brings opportunities for their tastes and demands. In this way the reference staff and its service can bring the right and the right book together. The third law expects this kind of service from the reference staff.

(iv) Popular Departments : To increase the change of every book getting its reader, creation of popular departments in the library is essential such as Magazine Section, Newspaper Reading Room. According to Dr. Ranganthan, the success of the third law depends on the law of probability to which more and more readers visiting the library will increase the changes of getting every book its reader.

(v) Publicity : Publicity is a powerful media of influencing and attracting the masses. Publicity can be useful and benefited to the library like that of other walks of life and social awareness. It can be helpful in making users of the library. They be conversant through press, publication news sheets, library bulletin annual reports, book week programmes, Radio-TV talks and public lectures etc. The library should adopt all recognized methods of attracting the public to the library. Thus, the principle of publicity enhance the chances for fulfillment of the third law.

(vi) Extension Service : The purpose of the extension is to convert the library into a social center to encourage the reading and to turn the non-readers into regular readers. The librarians educational function is to provide lectures, study circles, exhibitions should be organized. To satisfy the demand of the third law, the librarians should celebrate local such festivals celebrations which attract huge crowds of people. This form of extension service is essential to satisfy the cause of the third law.

(vii) Book Selection : Due attention is to be given to ascertain the tastes and needs of the readers. Suggestions of the users should be given due preference. Notes made by reference staff from day to day observation should be kept in mind. The book selection work be done taking into account the demands of the readers and the funds available.

4. Save the Time of the Reader

This law of library science has brought revolutionary reforms in the management of libraries. This law revolves round the readers. Like the Third Law, the Fourth Law also advocates open access. In libraries where the closed system is practised, the readers do not have access to books. They have to stand outside the stockroom with requisition of the books that they want. The procedure is that they prepare a list of the books that they want after consulting the catalogue, and hand over the list to a member of the staff. He may bring some of the books asked for and report non-availability of others. The reader, on actually seeing the books, may find that non of them answer his needs. He will have to prepare another list and again wait. This trial and error process may have to be repeated several times and yet his needs may not be fully met. A lot of time is spent in the process.

But in the open access system, the reader is engaged in handling and perusing the books and he is not conscious of the passage of time. So a lot of his subjective time is saved. If the books are properly arranged and there is no misplacement of books, his objective time is also saved. So open access is an effective means of satisfying the fourth law. Some other means of achieving the goals of this law are :

(i) Shelf Arrangement : The most common approach of the reader to books is by subject than by authors. If the shelf arrangement is in the classified helpful sequence, the reader takes little time to take out the book from the shelf. So the 4th law demands classified arrangement of books on the shelf. The relative classified of accommodation on the shelves should be closest possibility in the classified order. Apart from the relative position, the absolute position of the classes must be borne in the mind to meet the challenge of the 4th law. The class of the books that is in great demand should be shelved the nearest book shelves of the stock area and the class of books with little demand should be placed at the farthest end. This broken order will save the time of the reader.

(ii) Stack room Guides : In addition to the relative arrangement of the books, the librarian should provide well throughout the guides in the stack room in order to save the time of the reader falling which the reader is likely to waste much of his time in locating the shelves of the books of his interest. It will be useful to keep at the entrance, the whole plan of that room mentioning the position of the racks and the classes of books contained in the every row should have a signal guide and shelf guides alongwith to save the time of the readers. The stack room guides alongwith the proper placing of tags will enable readers to select books in no time.

(iii) Classification and Catalogue : Proper classification which would bring together books on a specific subject, a catalogue designed to meet the various approaches of readers, and reference service, stack room guides are all basic tools for securing fulfillment of this law. Adoption of an acquisition system that would ensure the speedy procurement of books and periodicals is also necessitated by this law.

(iv) Issue System : An important library operation which was not mentioned in the context of the earlier laws, but which has great relevance for this Law is the loan of books i.e., the issuing system. The earlier practice in libraries was to enter all books lent out in a register and their return to be recorded in the same register. There are some libraries still following this system but needless to say that this is a time consuming process and is not an evidence of the library paying deference to the Fourth Law. It is as a result of efforts to simplify this process and to reduce the time involved in the operation that the mode issue systems like the ticket system, photo-charging system and computer charging system have been evolved. In these modern systems there is substantial reduction of time in the issue and return process and so the Fourth Law strongly advocates them.

(v) Bibliography : Library catalogue enables a reader to locate the book without any loss of time but many micro thought appearing in the form of articles in the periodicals, pamphlets. The reader has no knowledge of the name of the author. He only knows the name of the subject. The time of the reader can be saved if the catalogue has the subject analytical entries. Besides, the library must acquire subject bibliographies, cumulative indexes of periodicals and bibliographies of Bibliographies etc.

(vi) Reference Service : Inspite of a good classified arrangement, an elaborated will prepared catalogue and bibliographical sources, may not be feasible for an average reader to locate his information. This needs the provision of trained staff to initiate to establish the contact between the reader and the document. The reference staff who is well acquainted with the catalogue and indexes and can handle them with greater ease and speed. Thus, the reference staff is the person who can bring together the book and the reader by rendering direct personal aid. The 4th law recommends both ready reference and long range reference services. Ready reference service is the reference service finished in a moment. Time is the very soul of ready reference service. It is also called fact finding service. Long range reference service expects the staff to conduct literature search on behalf of the reader. It involves scanning of the bibliographical documents and the original documents.

(vii) Library Location : The 4th law keeps in mind the time taken by the reader to reach the library. It should be located as to save the time of the reader. It should be at the central place to provide easy accessibility. The 4th law impacts that the branch libraries in the big cities should be located so that every citizen may find the library within ten minutes walk from the residence.

5. Library is a Growing Organism

The Fifth Law states "Library is a Growing Organism." The word used is 'Organism' and not 'organisation', which is significant, for it underlines certain characteristics of the library as a living organism. The fifth law implies that the objects of the growth in a library are its collection, space, readers and staff. As a growing organism takes in new matter, casts off old matter, changes in size and takes new shapes and forms, similarly, the fifth law invites our attention to the fact that the library as an institution has all the attributes of a growing organism.

The basic components of a library are (i) the books stock (ii) the staff (iii) the readers and (iv) the physical plant i.e., the building, furniture and equipments. When we say that a library grows what we mean is that each of these components grows. The implications of the fifth law are as under :

(i) Book Stock : In the initial stages the growth of the book stock including periodicals would be fast. This has its impact on the size of the stack room, the catalogue cabinet and the catalogue room and the number of racks for accommodating the books. All these will necessarily have to grow in number and/or in physical dimensions. Also, as the book stock grows and the newly added books are interpolated in the classified arrangement, there will be constant movement of books on the shelves. This would necessitate relabelling of shelves periodically. The stack room guides also will need to be periodically replaced by new ones to indicate the correct position of the changed arrangement of books.

(ii) Readers : The readers of the library are also bound to grow especially in a library that functions in keeping with the spirit of the first four laws of library science. This means that more reading space will be required.

(iii) Staff : Corresponding to the increase in the book collection and the number of readers, new services will have to be introduced. Depending on the nature and interests of readers, the services will also have to be diversified. Reference service will have to be intensified. New information services backed by modern technology will have to be introduced. There will be quantitative increase in administrative work and services and qualitative diversification of services. These would necessitate an increase of staff at different levels both in the quantitative and qualitative sense.

(iv) Physical Plant : The collection of the library should grow in keeping in view the space available at the disposal of the library. Space is always limited, it would increase in a limited extent. It can be said that the size of the space be bigger to house the collection and the collection may be grown in keeping in view of the space. While planning and designing a library building there should be provision for the expansion of the building both horizontally and vertically. The need for more space often arises much sooner than anticipated and the lack of provision for expansion would block its development.

(v) Casting off the old : As the growth in the collection is unavoidable, it is necessary to weed out old obsolete, unused and torn books to provide space for the new additions. Weeding out need not necessarily means the removal of the books from a library where their relevance has ceased, in order to make room for current and relevant books. Such books may be stored where they are available for occasional use. Different libraries in one area can store such books at a central place. This can be one of the areas of cooperation among libraries. This principle does not apply to the national library of a country or deposit libraries. It is necessary to preserve valuable materials from decay by lamination etc. methods in such libraries.

Concluding, it can be said that the present state of the libraries in the country is not much appreciable if consider from the point of view of the five laws but we realize that most of libraries have now adopted open access, classified arrangement on shelves, technical processing of the documents in consonance with the demands of the five laws. Thus, the five laws have revolutionized the field of libraries.

4
Library Movement

Q. : Describe the library movement in India.

or

Write an essay on the library movement in modern India.

Ans. India is known for its rich tradition of scholarship and learning and for cultural heritage. In ancient and medieval periods, there existed famous libraries around learning centres and places of religious worship. The rulers of the land in the medieval period had taken a deep interest in setting up libraries. During the sixteenth century, the work of Christian missionaries and introduction of printing had led to the establishment of some libraries. However, the library movement in India may be regarded to have had a proper beginning only after the advent of the British in the modern period. When English was introduced into the country and the British began to set up some modest educational facilities in the later half of the last century, libraries, in modern sense, began to spring up in some places in the country, notably in the provincial capitals. It was only after the country attained independence and the five year plans began to be implemented, that library development got attention in the country.

The library movement in India can be divided into following four periods :

1. Ancient Period
2. Mediaeval Period
3. Pre-Independence Period
4. Post-Independence Period

1. Ancient Period

The important centres of learning in ancient India as Nalanda, Vikramshila, Odantapuri, Somapuri, Jaggadal, Mithila, Vallabhi, Kanheri etc., had famous libraries attached to them.

Nalanda University (in Bihar) had its own multistoreyed library in 600 A.D. with massive collection of manuscripts in three buildings. Chinese traveller Hiuen-tsang visited this library in seventh century.

Vikramshila University had massive collection of manuscripts on tantras and Taxila University library had rare collection of manuscripts on agriculture and archery. Banabhatt managed the palatial library of King Bhoja.

2. Medieval Period

The Mughals had also set up royal and pompour libraries during their reign. The first Mughal emperor Babur was a voracious reader, prolific writer and a great lover of manuscripts. Humayun set up in Agra fort a library which was managed by Lal Beg. Similarly Akbar also set up a library under the control of Sheikh Faizi. Akbar converted the library of Agra fort in a rich library. He introduced reforms in the classification and storage of books.

Other rulers and kings also patronized libraries. Among them the names of Maharaja Sawai Man Singh of Jaipur and Maharaja Ranjit Singh of Punjab will be remembered with appreciation in the history of library service in India. Among other important contribution, is the Saraswati Mahal library established by Maharaja of Tanjaur.

3. Pre Independence Period

When the British established their rule and started settling in big colonies in this country, felt the need of libraries. The residents of Calcutta made an appeal to the Society for the promotion of Christian Knowledge to establish a 'circulating library' to meet their reading demands. The Society had conceded to their request and set on in the year 1709. The concept of 'libraries for all' had dawned on this soil. Subsequently a number of such libraries were established in this country. Notable among them are fort St. George Library (1714), East India Company's Library, Bombay (1715); Johan Andrews Circulating Library at Fort williams, Calcutta (1770); the Calcutta Circulating Library started by Messrs Cock, Marxwell and Co. (1787); and the Calcutta Literary Society's Library (1818).

In nineteenth century, important developments have taken place for library movement. In 1808, Government of Bombay, initiated a proposal to register libraries with a facility to give copies of books published from "Funds for the encouragement of Literature".

The Calcutta Public Library came into existence in August, 1835, which was basically meant to serve the needs of public irrespective of ranks and classes. This library later grew in the Imperial Library (1903) and National Library (1948).

In 1867, Government of India enacted the Press and Registration of Books Act (XXV), under which the printer of a book was supposed to deliver free to the provincial government concerned one copy of the book and one or two more copies, if the provincial government so desired. The additional copies were to be transmitted to the Central Library.

Khuda Baksh Oriental Public Library (Patna) was established in 1876 by Maulvi Muhammad Baksh Khan with a collection of 1,500 manuscripts. In 1891, the library was opened to the public. In 1860, a small library was established by Jean Mitchel in Madras as a part of museum. It was opened to the public in 1896 and was named Connemera public Library. In 1948, it become state central library.

Some other important libraries set up in the 19th century in India are Andrews Library, Surat (1850); Gaya Public Library, Gaya (1855), Long Library, Rajkot (1856), Government library, Junagarh (1867), Adyar Library, Adyar (1886), and Dahi Laxmi Library, Nadiad (1892).

The early part of the 20th century was considered as golden period in the history of public library movement in India. The contribution made by Maharaja Sayajirao III of Baroda to modern library movement in India is really remarkable. He introduced free primary compulsory education in his princely state in the year 1907. In 1908, while touring in America wired to his Prime-minister to open circulating libraries in villages of the Baroda State for diffusion of knowledge among the masses forthwith sanctioning Rs. 30,000 for this very project. The Education Department of the State thereupon worked out the scheme of establishing libraries in the state and offered Rs. 24 a year for periodicals, provided the villagers contributed a similar sum and also a set of new books worth Rs. 100 each on payment of Rs. 25 made by the people. He brought with him Mr. W.A. Borden from America for organizing the 'library system' of the State. Mr. Borden had established the State Central Library training classes and a journal by name *Library Miscellany.* He also designed a classification scheme suitable to the local needs and an alphabetical list of authours surnames. Children and Womens libraries were also established. By 1940-41, Baroda was covered by a network of about 1400 libraries.

Shiyali Ramamrita Ranganathan made significant contribution towards public library movement in India. The first Library Association formed in India was Desa Library Association of 1914. Soon after its formation the Association had compiled a *Directory of Andhra Libraries* and started the publication of its monthly organ *Granthalaya Sarvaswamu* in 1915. They had also organized library training classes and the All India Public Library Association in 1919. Of the various activities which the association had carried out in the early days, the 'library pilgrimages' can be regarded as unique and superb.

In 1915, Punjab University invited an American, A.D. Dickinson to reorganize its University library. He prepared a "prime of librarian," the first book on library science published in India. The first all India public library conference took place at Madras in 1919 and as a result All India Public Library Association came into being. This association organised conferences between 1919-34 but later became defunct.

The Indian Library Association was founded in the year 1933 with its headquarters in Calcutta. In the earlier years, it had compiled a directory of libraries and encouraged training of library personnel in the country. It had organised conferences in alternative years. In 1943, it had started its quarterly organ the *Library Bulletin*.

In 1937, University of Madras started a one year course leading to Postgraduate Diploma in Library Science.

4. Post Independence Period

Due to the efforts of Dr. Ranganathan, Madras (Tamil Nadu) became the first state of India which has library legislation.

Delhi public library was set up in 1951 as a model public library as a pilot project of UNESCO and INSDOC in 1952.

In the first five year plan (1951-56) of Indian Government the objective was to set up a National Central Library, and the State Central Libraries in each state, along with a network of circulating consisting of deposit stations and mobile vans in villages. By the end of the plan period, there were nine State Central Libraries and about 100 district libraries.

In 1954, Government of India passed the delivery of books act which later amended in 1956 and included newspapers also. This made compulsion for every publisher to send at his own cost to the National Library at Calcutta as well as to each of three public libraries at Delhi, Bombay and Madras.

During the second five year plan (1956-61), an amount of Rs. 140 lakhs was provided to the states for library development.

In 1957, Advisory Committee for libraries was set up under the chairmanship of Shri K.P. Sinha. The Committee submitted its report in 1958. It recommended 25 year library plan, levy of cess of 6 naye paise in a rupee on property tax; Government of India should contribute matching grant equal to cess collection by a state; each state should enact state library act and Government of India should enact central library act.

Hyderabad state enacted Hyderabad Public Libraries Act in 1955. This became defunct due to the merger of Hyderabad with other states. Andhra Pradesh Public Libraries Act 1960 came into force in 1960.

During the third five year plan (1962-67/69), the goal was to cover the entire country by means of a network.

The fourth five year plan was implemented in 1969-74. The Planning Commission set up in 1964 a 'working group on libraries' under the chairmanship of V.K.R.V. Rao. The group formulated overall policies, priorities, and programmes of public library development and estimated the cost of Rs. 30.99 crores.

Karnataka was the third state to enact library legislation in 1965 and after it Maharastra public libraries act was enacted in 1967, and West Bengal public libraries act in 1979.

During the fourth plan period Raja Ram Mohan Roy Library Foundation (RRRLF) was also set up in 1972 as an autonomous organization under the Department of Culture, Ministry of Education (now Ministry of Human Resource Development) for the development of public libraries in the country. It provides grants for purchase of reading materials and for construction and extension of library building. Recently it has taken active part towards formulation of draft on national policy on library and information system.

In the seventh five year plan 1985-90, Planning Commission working group was constituted to give a report on "Modernization of Library Sciences and Informatics"

In 1985, a committee on National Policy on library and Information System was appointed by the Government of India, Department of Culture, to advise the government on the formulation of national policy, under the chairmanship of D.P. Chattopadhyay. The committee submitted its report in 1986.

In 1988, the libraries act was introduced in Manipur state and in 1989 in Kerala and Haryana state. Where as, in 1993, the public libraries acts were came into existence in Goa and Mizoram state.

At the request of Indian Library Association, Delhi, Dr. Venkatappaiah drafted the model public libraries act in 1989, Keeping in view the recent developments and experiences, this model act was discussed in the National Seminar on Library Legislation held at New Delhi 1990.

In the wake of recent developments in country such as, New Panchayat and Municipal acts, after amending the Constitution in 1992, releasing of UNESCO Public Library Manifesto in 1994, total literacy campaign, emerging necessity of information at all levels, the earlier model act of Dr. Venkatappaiah was revised as Model Library and Information Services Act in 1995. Recently, Gujarat Public Libraries Act (2001) and Orissa Public libraries Act have also been introduced, working of which is in progress.

There were other states in India which do not have library legislation, like Assam, Bihar, Madhya Pradesh, Jammu and Kashmir, Sikkim, Arunachal Pradesh, Delhi, Uttaranchal, Jharkhand, Chattisgarh, but they have good libraries and network of libraries. These states also contributed a lot in the development of library movement in India.

As far as the academic libraries are concerned, today there are about 6,00,000 primary schools, 80,000 secondary schools and 400 universities in India. All the universities have good library facilities, their collection range from few thousands to a million. The growth of the libraries of universities is very rapid on account of the generous grants from the UGC, but the school libraries, on the whole have been neglected lot.

The special libraries have progressed well in their development, as a corollary to growth in science and technology, education and research and industrial and economic development. The number of special libraries in the country may be placed at 2,000 to 2,500 at present. They belong to fields such as science and technology, medicine, agriculture, social sciences, arts and humanities.

Summing up it can be stated that the library movement in India has not taken strong roots. In the present context, it started from the 'Baroda' state in 1910 and after 1939, the movement deteriorated due to lack of support from state government. The library movement has been slow and sporadic. This is mainly due to lack of library legislation in different states and union territories and also at the national level.

At present a number of states have been considering the matter of libraries act but have not been able to pass it. It is essential that all the states and union territories bring forth a library legislation of the earliest. In addition, there should be library law at the national level.

A library law would provide adequate provision for financial requirements. This would make possible the establishment and proper maintenance of public library system.

While constraints are a way of life, there are challenges and opportunities for making a thrust in library development in the country. The government users, and the library professionals have to share the responsibility of laying a firm infrastructure for library service in the country.

Q. : Write short note on National Policy on Library and Information System (NAPLIS).

Ans. The Raja Rammohan Roy Library Foundation and Indian Library Association brought out separate drafts on national library and information policy in 1985. Both these drafts touched upon library and information science education.

The Department of Culture, Ministry of Human Resource Development, Government of India appointed in October 1985 a Committee of senior library scientists and other specialists, with Prof. D.P. Chattopadhayaya as Chairman and Dr. B.P. Barua as member Secretary to prepare a draft document on National Policy on Library and Information System. After a series of seminars, symposia and meetings, the Committee submitted to Government its report entitled "National Policy on Library and Information System – A Presentation" on 30 May 1986.

The main aims of the library and information policy are stated as follows:

(i) to foster, promote and sustain, by all appropriate means, the organization, availability and use of information in all sectors of national activity ;

(ii) to take steps for mobilizing and upgrading the existing library and information systems and services and initiating new programmes relevant to our national needs, taking advantage of latest advances in information technology ;

(iii) to encourage and initiate, with all possible speed, programmes for the training of library and information personnel, on a scale and of a calibre adequate to provide library and information services and to recognize their work as an important component of the quality and level of such services ;

(iv) to set up adequate monitoring mechanisms for ensuring rapid development of library and information facilities and services for meeting the information needs of all sectors and levels of the national economy ;

(v) to encourage individual initiatives for the acquisition and dissemination of knowledge and for the discovery of new knowledge in an atmosphere of intellectual freedom;

(vi) in general, to secure for the people of the country all the benefits that can accrue form the acquisition and application of knowledge; and

(vii) to preserve and make know the nation's cultural heritage in its multiple forms.

The draft policy document consists of 10 chapters, viz. Introduction, Objectives, Public Library System, Academic Library System, Special Libraries and Information Systems, National Library System and Bibliographical Services, Manpower Development and Professional Status, Modernization of Library and Information systems, General Professional Issues and Implementing Agencies and Financial Support. The document has five appendices. Each chapter, after setting out the objectives, makes some specific recommendations towards upgrading and coordinating the existing library and information system and services and information support. The chapter on Implementing Agencies makes a specific recommendation for constituting a National Commission for Libraries and Information Systems to oversee the implementation of the recommendations of the National Policy.

Thereafter, the Government of India setup an Empowered Committee again under the chairmanship of Professor D.P. Chattopadhyaya to assess the policy document and drew-up an action plan. The Empowered Committee submitted its report in March, 1988.

The recommendations of the Empowered Committee are :

— Constitution of a National Commission on libraries to play a major role in implementing the library policy and in the progress of library development ;

— Creation of an All India Library Service ;

— Active involvement of the Central Government in public library development in the state ;

— Public library development has also to be supported by agencies involved in social education, rural development, etc;

— University and College libraries are to be considered academic units and that senior library staff members should be regarded as members of the academic community ;

— The National Library of India, Calcutta should be strengthened;

— Development of a system of national libraries.

— The formulation and implementation of a National Policy on Library and Information System are epoch making measures in the library movement in the country.

If the policy recommendations are faithfully implemented, a new phase in library development in India towards a far better performance and achievement is sure to come about.

Q. : Write an essay on the library movement in UK and USA.

Ans. : Library movement in UK since the middle ages to the 18th century religion was a dominating force in Europe, led to the establishment of monasteries. In the monasteries, reading and writing were the main occupations of the clergy. This necessitated the establishment of libraries in monasteries. In England, in addition to the monasteries a few societies were established for the promotion of Christian Knowledge and for the propagation of the Gospel. Similar educational agencies came into being for the dissemination of knowledge amongst the poorer classes of people. The immediate result of this was the establishment of Sunday Schools. In these Schools, the subjects taught were not entirely religious, but evening lectures on a variety of subjects become common. This gave impetus to the publication of several of several journals on a variety of subjects.

Before the end of the 17th century, there was a marked difference in the British society. Education was advancing by 1700 A.D. There were more than 500 grammar schools and 460 charity schools.

Newspapers started appearing and circulation increased rapidly when government censorship was removed in 1694.

These developments tended to encourage the growth of reading habit. There was also a shift from religious subjects to secular subjects. Some of the magazines and dailies like *Tatler, Spectator,* and *Gentleman's Magazine* appeared in the first decade of the 18th century. In the words of Samuel Johnson, England had become "a nation of readers". These conditions paved the way of establishment of commercial circulating libraries, religious libraries, endowed libraries and book clubs or reading societies. The part played by these in creating necessary condition for the starting of public library movement may be discussed as under :

Commercial Libraries : These were run by the booksellers for their private profit. These came into being in a large number during the middle of eighteenth century existing almost every where, and were patronized mainly by women. According to Irwin, "it developed from the natural inclination of good booksellers to lend to their trusted customers volumes which they wished to examine before purchase". These had a considerable influence on publicity and demand for books, which helped to create literary climate and reading habits. These were of all sorts, good and bad.

Religious Libraries : According to the Report of the Select Committee on Public Libraries (1849), the public usefulness of the Cathedral libraries, the old town and parochial libraries, etc.., was exceedingly limited. Most of them were small and a few had any regular income. Most of them were small and a few had any regular income. In England, parochial libraries were also established early in the eighteenth century by Dr. Thomas Bray (1656-1730) and some of his friends. Many of them experienced a similar fate but there were nearly two hundred Parish libraries in existence in 1849. There were a few parochial libraries of more recent foundation which were accessible to the public. For example, the Library at Bewdley in Worcestershire was bequeathed in 1819 for the use of clergy and other respectable inhabitants, "as a public library".

Endowed Libraries : These libraries are created by the gift of an individual or group. The ones like Chetham's Library in Manchester (1653), Shepherd Library (1761) at Preston and Sterling Library (1761) at Glasgow, resembled to our concept of public library. At Salford in

1846 three parks were purchased by public subscription and the mansion in Peel Park was subsequently used as Public Library and Museum. E.R. Langworthy, Mayor in 1849, gave over 15,000 pounds during the following thirty years. This is another example of a public library.

Clubs or Societies : These are one of the type of subscription library, which also became quite popular in the later half of the eighteenth century. It did not require a librarian or extensive premises. These were different from subscription libraries in the following three ways :

(i) Its membership was small,

(ii) It did not attempt to build a permanent collection, the books being disposed off when they had served their purposes,

(iii) It served social and literary needs.

The origin of such clubs or societies were due to clergy. They seem to have been numerous both in England and in Scotland, more in number than subscription libraries.

From 1823, onwards rapid expansion took place and by 1863 there were nearly a thousand institutes in active operation throughout the country. The conditions in individual institutes varied; in some, library would be the main feature and a few others lectures might be the chief concern. Major collection of books were mainly scientific. The libraries attached to these institutes later formed a nucleus of public library stock in their respective places.

In real sense, the library movement actually started after the enactment of the Public Library Act of 1850. Earlier libraries were being treated as a social institution. The following were the leading forces for created necessary conditions for the growth and development of libraries:

— Increasing industrialization gave birth to the breakup of the class structure, the rise of common man and migration form rural areas to urban;

— Mass support for universal education and other developments;

— Developments in reading materials;

— Role played by pioneer libraries; and

— Individual's support.

In 1849, William Ewart, a member of Parliament for Dumfries

Burghs in Scotland, took up a proposal for the establishment of libraries freely open to public and persuaded parliament to set up. Ewart, with the help of their member of the parliament introduced the first Public Libraries Bill in 1850. So the first Public Libraries Act was finally passed on 30 July 1850. The 1850 Act was applicable to England and Wales only, which permitted adoption only by towns with 10,000 or more population.

The Act of 1850 had implemented the limitations regarding :

— kinds of authorities for adoption;

— method of adoption;

— amount of money to be spent; and

— the ways of spending money.

The Public Library Act of 1919 provided for the establishment of country library authorities. After that the trust began to make grant to the authorities towards books, book boxes, shelving and other equipment. This Act permitted the development of urban library service by removing the rate limitations.

After the world war, it was considered that libraries would require a new deal so that their full potentiality could be realized. The expansion of library services took place particularly the provision of lending library facilities by special collection schemes and the initiation of gramophone record lending libraries.

In 1957, the Ministry of Education set up a Committee, with Sir Sydney Roberts as its Chairman, "to consider the structure of the public library service in England and Wales". The report was published in 1959. The Public Libraries and Museum Act, 1964 resulted in a significant change of relationship between central government and public libraries in both England and Wales. For the first time the provision for "a comprehensive and efficient and efficient service" was made mandatory.

The Local Government Act 1972 led to the creation of fewer and larger library authorities. This step had led to a greater possibility for the provision of an efficient and comprehensive library service. These acts have drastically affected the patterns of development of library services in public libraries.

Library movement in USA

The development of libraries in USA is relatively of recent origin. Early migrants to America were more concerned in settling down and making a living. They were more anxious to build a house in the wilderness and to find an avocation. In spite of hazardous life of the early migrants they had not forgotten their religious heritage. The clergy had carried their bible and the physician his books, but by and large the early collection was mainly religious. Still then, some private libraries with a very modest collection came into being.

Some of the early settlers in America brought with them their private collection of books. Libraries in the Colonial Period were mainly private libraries. Some of the well known private libraries belonged to, William Brewster of Plymouth Colony; Johan Winthrop Governor of Connecticut; Col. William Byrd of Westover, Virginia; James Logan of Philadelphia. Their collections were between 3000 to 4000.

On the pattern of Book Clubs and subscription libraries, some libraries were also established in USA, which designated as special libraries. Benjamin Franklin was pioneer in starting social libraries. He floated a company in the year 1793 called Library Company of Philadelphia and requested interested persons to become members. The initial subscription was 40 shillings and an annual fee of 10 shillings, Franklin's library was often referred to as the mother of the social library in America.

Subscription libraries of varying sizes began to proliferate throughout USA. Three other well known subscription libraries were (i) Redwood Library of Newport, (ii) New York Society Library of New York city and (iii) Charleston Library Society of Charleston. Social libraries were very popular during the period 1790-1815 and thereafter there was a gradual decline due to the rise of public libraries supported by the state. One major feature of the subscription libraries was the nature of the library collection. This collection was quite different, with less emphasis upon religion and more upon secular matters, like history, biography, travel, literature, grammar, agriculture, arithmetic and natural science.

Before the advancement of the free public libraries a novel idea was mooted by the Governor of New York, Dewitt Clinton. He recommended to the State Legislature for the formation of School

District libraries. The idea was to house these libraries in the existing schools and open them for public without any charges.

There was one library set up that has given a lead to the nation, is the Library of Congress, which was established in 1800 by law to serve the information needs of the Congress. It is now the national library of USA.

In USA, first public library was formed in 1833. It was an important event in the history of public library movement in USA. Besides, the following broad social forces were responsible for the emergence of public libraries in USA.

— Public support for universal education,
— Increasing industrialization,
— Opening of the reading room,
— Contribution made by prominent persons,
— Interest and involvement of churches and religious groups.

Much of the credit for the development of libraries in USA has gone to the American Library Association, founded in the year 1876. The ALA constitution stated its objectives and spelled out in clear terms its goals and priorities. The ALA Policy Manual listed its priorities : (1) Access to information (2) Legislation/funding (3) Intellectual Freedom and (4) Public Awareness. The ALA's contribution to the development of public libraries is considerable.

Public libraries in the modern sense began to be established through local legislation in the second half of the 19th century. The public libraries began to expand their services to wards the last quarter of 19th century, by adding recreational reading and reference. In addition, service to children was also initiated. The aim being to attract all the citizens to the library, in order to educate them and also to improve the masses.

The public libraries in USA from 1960s onwards have moved actively to take reading materials and services to the people, even who were not habitual users of libraries. Special attention was given to minorities and disadvantaged persons. Reference and information services have been improved. The development of information technology has revolutionised the library system. Libraries have responded to multimedia, hyper media, CD-ROMs and information highway to serve as a resource centre for variety of users including industry and student community.

Library Services Act (LSA) in USA was enacted in 1956, as a result Federal government came into the picture for the first time. The Act was meant to assist in the establishment of library services in previously unserved areas specially rural areas. In 1960s, LSA was extended further for the five years. In 1964, The Library Services and Construction Act (LSCA) was passed, replacing LSA. The scope was broadened to cover funds for the construction and remodeling of library facilities. The word rural was deleted, whereby all public libraries became eligible for federal aid. Two conditions were added. According to it, each state was also required to prepare a comprehensive plan for the purpose of library development. LSCA has aimed at library development. LSCA has been amended over years to include federal support for public library construction; promotion of inter-library cooperation; and the improvement of services for disadvantaged people.

The LSCA includes four authorized titles as :

Title I – Public library services

Title II – Public library construction

Title III – Inter-library cooperation

Title IV – Older Reader Services.

LSA and LSCA have given a considerable impact on the growth and development of public libraries but fluctuations in funding have been rather unfortunate. In fact, there has been a great gap between what has been promised through legislative authorisation and appropriation. This has led to adhoc decision and difficulties during lean periods.

Concluding, it can be said that in both UK and USA early development of libraries was due to private efforts. Subscription and commercial libraries were common in both the countries. Religion played a dominant part and was responsible for the establishment of monastic and parochial libraries. Commerce and industry also gave impetus to starting the mechanics or mercantile libraries.

However, it was library legislation which gave a sound footing to the development of public libraries in both the countries. Legislation provided the much needed funds. Commissions and Committees appointed form time to time kept a watch on the improvement of library services. Another factor that was responsible for library movement was generous donations by philanthropists.

In both the countries the professional associations took keen interest for the improvement of libraries and gave directions in this regard. Thus, libraries become the true centres of learning.

5
National Library System of India

Q. : What are national libraries? Discuss in brief the working and functioning of a National Library.

or

What are the important objectives and functions of a National Library ? Discuss.

or

Discuss the objectives and functions of National Library of India.

or

Discuss the functions of a National Library. How far does the National Library of India fulfills these functions?

Ans. : A national library is the most comprehensive library which services a particular country's citizen. It is governed and funded by national government.

One of the unique privileges of a national library of a country is to receive by law all print and non-print materials produced by the country. This legal provision is usually incorporated in the Copyright Laws of the country, by which an author, an artist or a musician, has the exclusive right, granted by law, for a certain number of years, to make and dispose copies of a literary, musical or artistic work. These laws provide the government to receive a few copies of print and non-print materials which are usually deposited with the national library. Such legal privileges are also obtained for the national library of a country by special laws enacted for the purpose.

The national library is variously defined as under :

ALA Glossary of Library Terms defines a national library as a library maintained by a nation.

In 1970, UNESCO, in its recommendations concerning the International Standardization of Library Statistics adopted by the general conference at its 16th session, offered the following definition to the national library:

Libraries which, irrespective of their title, are responsible for acquiring and conserving copies of all significant publications published in the country and functioning as a "deposit" library, either by law or under other arrangements. They will also normally perform some of the functions: produce a national bibliography; hold and keep up to date a large and representative collection of foreign literature including books about the country; act as a national bibliography; hold and keep up to date a large and representative collection of foreign literature including books about the country; act as a national bibliographical information centre; compile union catalogues; publish the retrospective national bibliography.

Libraries which may be called "national" but whose functions do not correspond to the above should not be placed in the "national libraries" category.

Edition 6 of *Harrod's Librarians Glossary and Reference Book* (1987), defines the national library in the following words :

(i) a library maintained out of government funds ;

(ii) serving the nation as a whole ;

(iii) usually, books in such libraries are for reference only ;

(iv) they are usually copyright libraries ;

(v) the functions of such a library is to called and preserve for posterity, the books, periodicals, newspapers and other documents published in the country; this is best done by a law requiring publishers to deposit copies of all publications issued by them ; and by

(vi) purchasing books published in other countries.

The definition of the national library given by UNESCO is more comprehensive and covers most important functions of a national library.

Objectives and Functions of National Library

The early national libraries had some specific features which justified their existence. These includes :

1. Their traditional functions are those of acquisition, storage and organization for the use of the most complete set of national printed output. There is no doubt about the importance of these functions in the present situation.
2. Over decades and even centuries, the national libraries have accumulated general collections of foreign literature which no other library in the country can match.
3. These holdings consist of literature covering some spheres of knowledge for which there are no independent special libraries. They also have rare language publications which cannot be handled in other libraries due to lack of personnel familiar with these languages.
4. Lastly, at the present stage of library service development the need is all the more acute in centralization, standardization and coordination of library activity, both within the country and on an international scale. It is thus best to entrust the implementation of these problems to he national library - with a rich collection and rich reference facilities, sufficiently financed and with qualified personnel.

Over the years the functions and priorities of a national library have been reviewed by several experts. After due assessment and reassessment of the priorities, one important aspect emerges is that of the role of leadership by the national libraries. A national library can set the tune for the other libraries in the country as a good national library system cannot function without a National Library. The National Library is a physical manifestation of the national library service.

Broadly speaking, the functions of a national library can be studied under following perspectives:

— Collection Development

— Disseminating Information

— Preparation of National Bibliographies

— Reader's Services

1. Collection Development

These functions are spelled out below :

(i) To serve as a central and comprehensive collection of national output, acquired through legal deposits, gifts or exchange;

(ii) To acquire and maintain documents about the country or its people or activities, published outside the country by any national or in any language or form;

(iii) To collect and preserve select manuscripts and such other archival records of national relevance and importance;

(iv) To collect foreign documents for which there may be demanded from the people of the country;

(v) To collect and preserve specialized materials such as books for the blind, dramatic compositions, engravings, medals, music compositions, cinematic films, photographs, sound recordings, etc., if these materials are not being collected by other agencies;

(vi) In sum, conserving the national intellectual and cultural heritage for the benefit of the future.

2. Disseminating Information

The information on books, periodicals and other materials collected may have to be disseminated through :

(i) Catalogues in printed, microforms and computer readable forms:

(ii) Compilation of retrospective or current bibliographies on various subjects in anticipation of or on request.

Retrospective bibliographies include past publications over a period of time, while current ones confine only to current publications. Current bibliographies are usually complied on request from scholars and institutions on current topics, most of which may be short and selective.

(iii) Index to currently published journals literature appearing in research and/or scholarly periodicals, if no other institution or agency complies and publishes indexes to current scholarly or research journals.

(iv) Preparation and production of abstracts of current literature on subjects of national interest.

3. Preparation of National Bibliographies

Preparation and production of national bibliographies of books and periodicals and other non-print materials, in printed and/or microforms and computer readable forms is also done by national libraries. By-products of these may be directories of publishers, authors of repute with their addresses and current statistics relating to production of books and other documents.

4. Reader's Services

These may include :

(i) Providing facilities for reading, consulting, etc. on the premises, including research alcoves/rooms for serious readers such as researchers, scholars and writers;

(ii) Offering reference, bibliographic and information services;

(iii) Providing inter-library lending and serving as a national and international inter-library loan centre;

(iv) Providing photocopying services, including the preparation of slides, overhead transparencies and other facilities to scholars, researchers and others;

(v) Offering specialised services to government, business and industries such as answering technical enquires from business and industry, preparation of special lists/bibliographies on specific topics on request from government departments;

(vi) Serve as referral centre, which assists users to locate any source of information through specialized directories and guides.

National Library of India

The constitution of India provides for the establishment of a National Library under article 62 of the VII Schedule of the Union List, and declared it as an institution of National importance. The history of our National Library can be seen in three distinct phases as under :

Phase I : 1835-1903 – Calcutta Public Library

The beginning of the present National Library can be traced to the Calcutta Public Library founded by public men and scholars of Calcutta in 1835. In 1844, the Calcutta Public Library moved into a spacious building, built in honour of Lord Metcalf, the then Governor-General. In 1857, consequent on the outbreak of the Indian War of

Independence, the Europeans of Calcutta withdrew their support for the library and the Calcutta Municipality stepped in to fill the vacuum and took over the management of the library in 1859.

Phase II : 1903 1947 – The Imperial Library

In 1899, when Lord Curzon, the then Viceroy and Governor General of India, visited the library, he found it in a miserable condition. Lord Curzon, who was interested in art and learning, immediately swung into action. He bought the rights of the library from the proprietors and later merged this library with the Official Imperial Library consisting of government departmental libraries and the remnants of the East India Company Library. With this nucleus, Lord Curzon declared open the new Imperial Library of India on 30th January 1903 in the Metcalf Hall. John Mc Farlane of the British Museum was invited to look after the new imperial library.

The Government of India in 1928 appointed a committee under the chairmanship of Mr. J.A. Richey for the administrative reorganization of the library. Among other recommendations, this committee felt that the Imperial Library should be declared as a copyright depository library. The successive librarian followed up this recommendation for many years. Finally, the Delivery of Books (Public Libraries) Act, 1954 could realise their efforts. In 1935, library training courses too were started in the Imperial Library, Calcutta.

Phase III : 1948-Present - the National Library of India

After India got its independence, the nation builders transformed the existing Imperial Library into the National Library of India in 1948. One of the most pressing needs of the library was additional space. This problem was solved by a magnanimous gesture which the then Governor-General of India, Sri C. Rajagoplachari, made by offering the Viceroy's Palace in Calcutta, namely, the Belvedere Palace, with its sprawling, lush green lawns for housing the new National Library. Shri B.S. Kesvan a man of vision, enthusiasm and administrative skill was appointed as a Librarian into a temple of knowledge of free India. This new National Library was opened to the nation in February 1953 by Maulana Abul Kalam Azad which marked the golden jubilee of the previous Imperial Library.

The library operates on an annual budget approved by the Government of India for the acquisition of materials, staff salaries, equipment and services. Presently, the library has a staff strength of over 800 persons which includes library professionals, language specialists and subject specialists. The Ministry of Education, Government of India appointed a Review Committee in 1969 and this committee recommended the following basic features of the National library.

1. Organisation and Management : The National Library is a department of the Ministry of Human Resources Development. The Director is the head of the Institution, assisted by two professional librarians. There are also deputy and assistant librarians to look after the technical and professional work of the library. Two administrative officers assist the Director in administrative matters.

The library is organized on a functional basis. The technical and professional functions operate under two main divisions viz. Professional and Conservation. The professional divisions now 42 in number, look after acquisition, processing, maintenance of reading materials and readers services. Divisions of reprography, preservation and laboratory, functions come under the conservation division. The administrative division is concerned with personnel, maintenance of building and garden, security, etc. Except for the Laboratory division which is headed by a Chemist and the Reprography division under the joint supervision of an Assistant Librarian and a Microphotographer, all the other technical divisions are headed by Assistant Librarians. The Organisational charts Fig. 1 (A&B) of the library gives an idea of the organizational set up of the Library.

The library is currently housed in four buildings, three of which are at the Belvedere Palace and the fourth at Esplanade. The Belvedere place has sprawling, lush green lawns which make the building look picturesque.

2. Collection : The National Library has a collection of nearly 23 lakh books and other reading materials. The collection is built up through :

— Books received through the Delivery of Books Act;

— Purchase

— Gifts

— Exchange

— Depository privileges

The majority of books are in English and in the Indian languages and the rest in a few foreign languages. It has some notable gift collections which have enriched its holdings very considerably. Some of the outstanding gifts have been the collections of Sir Asutosh Mukherji (76,000 books), Ramdas Sen, Barid Baran, Judunath Sarkar, Dr. S.N. Sen, Vaiyapuri Pillai and the archival papers of Sir Tej Bahadur Sapru. The pride of place in these gifts go to Sir Asutosh collection, which covers the whole gamut of subjects in the humanities and in the sciences as far as knowledge extended upto the early decades of the 20th century.

Being a repository for United Nations documents and its agencies, the library has a rich collection of United Nations publications. According to arrangements made without government, also received are government publications from Great Britain, America, Canada and European Economic Community publications.

3. Processing of Publications : All the books are classified according to the Dewey Decimal Classification scheme, catalogued according to Anglo-American Cataloguing Rules (AACR-II) and for providing subject headings in Dictionary Catalogue, the Library of Congress Subject Heading is used. For assigning the author marks, Cutter's Three Figure Author Table is used. The library catalogue is both in the card and printed forms. The Card Catalogue is in the dictionary form for English language publications, arranged in two sequences, author and subject.

The printed catalogue of the library is available in 10 volumes which is the alphabetical author catalogue, covering authors names beginning with the letters A to S.

4. Reader's Services : The National Library has following services for its users.

— Lending services
— Reading rooms
— Bibliography and Reference service
— Reprography service

(a) *Lending Services* : The National Library is unique in the sense that all books, expect rare publications, gifts, out of print books, government and United Nations publications and serials, are lent to the members. Although the collection of the national libraries is usually for reference purposes only, this library, for historical reasons, has continued lending facilities to its members. As part of lending services, inter-library loan service is also available to its members and institutions. For this assistance is taken from several national and international information institutions.

(b) *Reading Rooms* : The main reading room of the library has a seating capacity of over 300 persons and stocks over 10,000 general reference works on several fields of knowledge. In addition to this, there are 10 more reading rooms for use of various specialised materials.

(c) *Bibliography and Reference Service* : The bibliography and reference service is offered to satisfy the requirements of scholars, researchers and other users for a bibliography on a specific topic. There is no charge for this service and only short and selective bibliographies are supplied.

Besides, National Library also brings out retrospective bibliographies on subjects of national interest. The Central Reference Library compiles and publishes the Indian National Bibliography, a monthly record of Indian Books on the basis of publications received by the National Library under the Delivery of Books and Newspapers (Public Libraries) Act.

Reference Services are offered to users not only by personally answering the queries but also by telephone and by post or e-mail etc.

(d) *Reprography Services* : The various reading rooms are equipped with xerox facilities which provide photocopies of journal articles and technical reports or the users at a nominal rate. As part of the modernization process, wider range microfilming of materials is also carried out as for preservation, storage and retrieval for the future.

An in-house printing unit is operating for printing small documents for limited circulation.

5. Budget : The National Library operated with an annual budget of Rs. 40 lakhs, appropriated by the government, in 1984-85, of which Rs. 14.25 lakhs were spent on the purchase of books.

6. Staff : The National Library has a staff strength of about 800, a third of which being library professionals and the rest having other specializations.

On comparing with other major national libraries of the world, India's National Library is in its infancy. In 1968, the Government of

Fig. 1-A : Organisational Chart, National Library, Calcutta

Director		Librarian................		Librarian(II)..................
Deputy Librarian (I)	**Deputy Librarian (IV)**	**Deputy Librarian (V)**	**Deputy Librarian (II)**	**Deputy Librarian (III)**
1. All Indian Languages Divisions and Sections	1. Acq. (Bok Se ection) Division	1. Annexe Stack & Reading Room Division	1. Reading Room & Reference Division	1. Science & Technology Division
2. West Asian and African Languages Division	2. Acq. (Book Order) Division	2. Esplanade Reading Room	2. Stack Division (including New Stack)	2. Laboratory Division
3. East Asian Languages Division	3. English Serials Divisions	3. F.O.D. Division	3. Lending Section	3. Preservation Division
	4. English Processing Division	4. I.O.D. Division Division	4. Bibliography (Special)	4. Reprography Division
	5. Printed Catalogue Division	5. Maps & Prints Division	5. Bibliography (Special) Division	5. Stock Verification Division
	6. Co-ordination Division	6. Gift & Exchange Division	6. Children's Library	6. Rare Books Division
	7. Extension Training and Statistics	7. Asutosh Collection	7. Slavonic Languages	7. Gardens Division
	8. Exhibition Section		8. Germanic Languages Division	
			9. Romance Language Division	
			10. Holiday Duty	

Senior Administrative Officer	**Administrative Officer (I)**	**Administrative Officer (II)**	**Security Officer**	**Hindi Cell**
	Establishment Section, General Section, Central Registry Section, Public Relations Sections.	Accounts Section, Supply & Services, Cash Section,	Security and Conservancy Division	Hindi Officer implementation official language Act and Hindi teaching scheme, Hindi work.

Fig. 1-B: Technical Divisions of the National Library, Calcutta, India

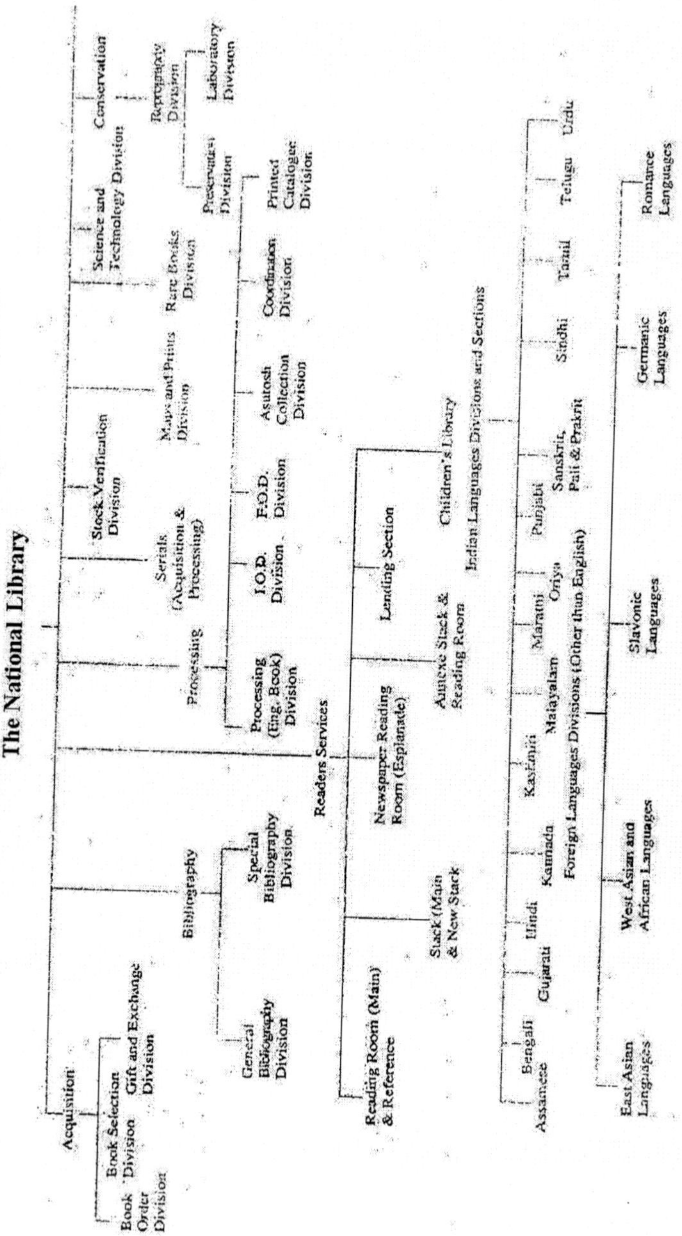

India appointed a committee of eminent educationists to review the working of the national library and to make recommendations for its further development. Valuable suggestions have also been given by experts from time to time to modernize the activities of the national library and bring it to the level of well-established national libraries of the world.

As part of an elaborate modernization plan, most of the library operations have been automated or are in the process of being automated. Various modern technologies have been introduced which include latest computer systems, networking, introduction of CD-ROM technology, DTP system for publications, etc. The staff is also being trained to handle the modern technologies.

6
Library Legislation

Q. : What do you mean by library legislation? Describe the needs for library legislation.

or

Justify the relevance of library legislation in present day context.

or

What is library legislation? Discuss the need and purpose of library legislation in India.

or

Explain the need for library legislation. Identify the essential components of a model public library act.

or

Discuss the sailent features of the library acts passed so far in India.

or

What is public library act? Discuss any of them in context of India.

Ans. : The Public Library is a social establishment concerned with the public and their educational, social and cultural activities. Its existence is very much essential for the socio-economic development of a country. It is crucial for the public library to demonstrate that the services rendered are worth against the money spent on it, because every rupee of its expenditure is obtained by the members of the community. This emphasizes that every one has a right to know about, and the right to use, public libraries. For the development of library services in any country, it is essential that there should be a statutory law. A law helps in creating necessary conditions, under which public libraries in the modern sense can be established and maintained adequately to serve the needs of users.

Commenting upon the need of Library Legislation UNESCO Public Library manifesto (1994) states that :

"Public Library is the responsibility of local and national authorities. It must be supported by specific legislation and financed by National and Local Government."

The library legislation provisions depend upon the social, cultural, political and economic conditions. A library law should provide legal basis for :

(i) Structure of library systems,

(ii) Establishment and maintenance of library systems,

(iii) Proper government and management,

(iv) Financial support :

  (a) Annual budget allocation by the state out of its total funds, and

  (b) Income from library cess supplemented by means of grants from the state government.

Need for Library Legislation

A survey of public libraries reveals that almost all countries in the world have public libraries, wherein documents are provided for general reading, either free of charge or for small subscription. The public libraries were established all over the world by charitable institutions, educational, social and religious organisations including the philanthropists.

While reviewing the literature published on public libraries particularly during the past 4-5 decades one can find that the need for enactment of public library law has been considered is very much essential to develop public library services in a country on proper lines. In the countries like UK and USA, the public library law had been enacted almost 150 years ago. Looking into the recommendations of National and International organisations like UNESCO, IFLA, LA, ALA and ILA including the UNESCO public library manifesto (1949, 1972 and revised in 1994), almost all organised seminars and conferences on public libraries, it is seen that the deliberations of those seminars and several other important documents have emphasized that the public library should be established under the clear mandate of law and it should be maintained wholly from public funds. Therefore it can ensure that the nationwide provisions of public library service

In India the contributions of Dr. S. R. Ranganathan and few others and the recommendations of the Advisory Committee for libraries appointed by the Government of India in 1958. (Sinha Committee Report) Seminars, conferences, etc., at the national and regional levels have always emphasized the need for library legislation in each state and Union Territory. As a result, ten states viz., Tamil Nadu (1948), Andhra Pradesh (1960), Karnataka (1965), Maharastra (1967), West Bengal (1979), Kerala (1989), Manipur (1988), Haryana (1989), Mizoram (1993), and Goa (1993) have not only already passed public library act but they have also made a significant progress and the development of public library services in their own states.

The enactment of a public library act undoubtedly ensures enormous advantages for the overall progress of the public library system. It is in the interest of proper growth and better functioning of these libraries. Broadly speaking, the library legislation is needed because :

1. It constitutes a proper administrative and supervisory body with executive powers;
2. It provides a well organised library system for the state, district and put the remote village level with free access to all the citizens;
3. It provides a steady and permanent source of finance;
4. It maintains standards in library service; and
5. It obliges to meet the objectives and remain accountable.

Finally, it is to be noted that library and information service is a crucial factor in the national development for meeting learning needs of the masses.

This, it is only through a State Public Library Act that a public library system could be created, sustained and promoted, ensuring a smooth financial flow, properly governed and managed to provide modern library services to all.

Objectives of Library Legislation

The following are the three main objectives of public library legislation:

1. To preserve the resources giving reliable information and for recreation,

2. To organise them well to enhance their use, and
3. To attract non-users to be users and users to be purposive users.

Purpose of Library Legislation

Public Library is the product of modern democracy and a practical instrument of its faith in universal education of a life long process. The purpose of Library Legislation is to :

1. Create the necessary library agencies by the enactment of Library Laws.
2. Guarantee establishment of a network of libraries on statutory basis.
3. Ensure stable financial support on a progressive basis.
4. Set up library authorities, which are responsible for the staffing, administration and management of the libraries.
5. Ensure permanent, uniform, efficient, expanding and co-ordinated library service, and
6. Presuppose free services and make it easily accessible to potential users irrespective of their qualification and age.

Functions of Library Legislation

The function of Library Legislation are as follows:

1. Define vividly the responsibility of the government in the set up and maintenance of public libraries.
2. Constitute and function the library at national, state and local level.
3. Provide a stable basis for library finance either by a special cess or by reservation of a certain percentage of budget for public libraries in the education budget.
4. Outline the structure of the public library system in the state.
5. Provide change for active participation of the public through representatives at the functioning of publication libraries at all levels.

Components of Library Legislation

The Public Libraries Act, which is to be operated in Indian conditions should have the follow components:

1. **Preamble :** The preamble, of the Act should clearly spell out

the objectives of library legislation and therefore, it should be precise and explicit.

2. **State Level Authority:** The Act should have the provision for the constitution of a Board as the State Library Authority,

   The Minister-in-charge of libraries should be the State Library Authority, charged with the duty of implementing the Act. It will be his duty to supervise and promote the improvement of the library service, provided by the library authorities and to secure proper discharge of their functions. It shall be his statutory duty to establish, equip administer a State library system, providing comprehensive and efficient library service free of charge, to all the citizens in the state.

3. **Chief Executive of the State:** In this Act, the Chief Executive at state level shall be called the Director of Public Libraries, who should an in information science professional. The Director shall supervise and control the public library system of the state with the guidance of the State Library Authority.

4. **Network of Libraries:** The act should provide for establishment and functioning of public libraries as a pyramidal structure from village, or even a hamlet level, to the state level via the districts covering towns and tehsils, etc.

5. **Financial Clauses :** The Act should spell out financial sources to ensure a regular of funds and their deployment. There should be a provision in the Act to collect library cess from all possible sources. Dr. S.R. Ranganathan, a pioneer in library legislation in India, advocated for the provision of library cess in the Model Acts, he incorporated the provision of library cess in all Acts he had drafted in his lifetime. The Advisory Committee for Public Libraries headed by Shri K.P. Sinha, examined this issue and opined that "in spite of a strong body of opinion against library cess, the committee has come to the conclusion that only a cess can provide a stable base for library finance." It is to be recognised that the levy of library cess is essential for a planned and systematic growth of an authority through assured and established financial resources.

6. **Manpower:** A provision should be made to create a cadre of State Library Service, and all the members of the said service should be Government servants, and their recruitment and

conditions of service should be as per provisions of the Article 309 of the Constitution of India.

7. **Accountability:** The activities and accounts of the Public Library System shall be open to public inspection, supervision and as per official audit rules.
8. **Registration of Books:** There must be a provision for the registration of books and periodicals published in the state under the legal deposit rules.
9. **Rules:** Rules should be made by the State Library Authority for all the sections and for smooth functioning, administration and control of the offices and the staff.

Efforts by the Government of India

The Government of India constituted the National Central Library Committee in 1948 and Dr. S.R. Ranganathan presented a draft Union Library Bill with a 30 years development plan for consideration of this committee.

The transformation of the former Imperial Library into the National Library of the country in 1948, the establishment of the Delhi Public Library with the assistance of UNESCO, 1951, the passing of the Delivery of Books Act in 1954, amended to cover periodical publication in 1956, all these constituted acts of great foresight of Central Government of free independent India. The Union Government also appointed a Library Advisory Committee in 1957 under the Chairmanship of Sinha. The Sinha committee favoured and supported for the enactment of Library Legislation in India in general and the states in particular. As a follow up of the recommendations of this committee, the central government set up in 1959 a committee under the chairmanship of Dr M.D Sen to frame a Model Public Library Bill. The committee submitted its report with a model bill in 1962. In 1963, the union government circulated the draft library bill widely among the states and Library Association. It was in 1972 Central Government of India established RRRLF to assist the proper development of public libraries in the country. It is the right time of the central government of India the RRRLF should be strengthened financially to enable it to discharge its responsibilities effectively.

The most important decision not towards the Library Legislation but for the overall development of library and information systems in

India was the appointment of a committee in -1986 by the HRD Ministry on National Policy on Library and Information systems. The report is already submitted by the committee to the government. In this, most important task before the government suggested to the government is, to establish, maintain and strengthen the free public libraries in the country and enable them to work as a system. This is possible only through the enactment of Library Legislation at the National Level and to support and encourage all the State Government.

Current Status

Several attempts were made by individuals and library associations to provide public libraries under law. Apart from Dr. S.R. Ranganathan, a number of individuals lent their time and energy to put on the statute book public library laws. Notable among them are, Kumar Munindra Deb Rai Mahasai of Bengal, K.V. Krishna Swamy Iyer, T.R. Venkataraman Sastry, Basheer Ahmed Sayeed of Madras, M.V. Donde of Bombay, K.M. Ujalambkar of Hyderabad and P.M. Kaula of Delhi.

It is only after India's independence that Dr. Ranganathan's dream of Public Library act enactment was fulfilled. Through the good offices of the then Minister for Education, Advinasilingam Chattier, a modified Bill was introduced in the state legislature which was passed as the Madras Public Libraries Act in 1949. Since then the following ten States have enacted library acts for their respective states:

1. Tamil Nadu (1948)
2. Andhra Pradesh (1960)
3. Karnataka (1965)
4. Maharashtra (1967)
5. West Bengal (1979)
6. Manipur (1988)
7. Kerala (1989)
8. Haryana (1989)
9. Goa (1993)
10. Mizoram (1993)

The salient features of the above mentioned acts are given under:

1. Tamil Nadu Public Libraries Act, 1948

This act was adopted in 1948. A Director of Public Libraries under the Control of Education Department use to control the public library service. Now it has been amended and the Director of Public Libraries is directly controlling the services of the public libraries in the state.

The sailent features of this act are :

(i) For the purpose of governing the Public libraries, a State Library Committee is to be formed. The State Education Minister is the President of the Committee. Its members include representatives of the Universities and local library authorities. The State Library Association sends three representatives to this Committee. The Director of Public Instruction would act as the Director of Public Libraries. A special officer assisting the Director in the administration of the Public Libraries under the Act is the Secretary to the Committee.

(ii) Local Library Authorities (LLA) are established in the City of Madras, and one each for various districts.

(iii) LLA has control over the cess to be collected by the local bodies such as corporations, municipalities, taluk boards and panchayats.

(iv) Each LLA has the power to make regulations for providing library services under its purview.

(v) Each LLA has to provide for the admission of the general public to Public Libraries in its area on such conditions and on payment of such fees as it may specify and require from persons, desiring to use such libraries, guarantee or security against injury to misuse, destruction, or loss of the property of such libraries.

(vi) Every local authority is empowered to levy a library cess in its area of 6 paise per rupee. This can be increased by the local authority after obtaining permission from the government.

(vii) One of the duties of the Director of Public Libraries is to declare which of the libraries are eligible for government aid. These libraries are other than those established under the Act which may lay down that the Director shall maintain a register of such libraries. Conditions are laid down for eligibility to receive government grants.

(viii) The Act provides for the contribution by the State Government to each local authority an amount not less than the cess collected by every local authority except that of the city of Madras.

(ix) The Act amended Section 9 of the Press and Registration of Books Act, 1857 to the effect that every printer shall deliver five copies of each book to the State Government out of which four will be deposited in the State Central Library.

(x) The Act also provides for a City Central Library for each city with a population of 50,000 or more with branch libraries and delivery stations added on as and when readership increases.

2. Andhra Pradesh Public Libraries Act, 1960

Andhra Pradesh Public Libraries Act, 1960, came into force with effect from April 1, 1960 which later amended in 1964 and 1969. This is the only state, which has a separate minister for public libraries. There is a state library committee with the minister as its chairman, which advises the government on all matters relating to the development of public libraries in the state. There is a separate Directorate of Public Libraries headed by the Director. The Director is the Secretary to the State Library Committee and is empowered to control the total affairs of the public library.

The sailent features of this act are :

(i) The Act defines the Public Library as a library maintained by the Government or any local body.

(ii) The local bodies have library authorities. It has more elected member than nominated members.

(iii) The State Library Committee is called State Library Council and has an elected member as the Chairman instead of the minister of libraries.

(iv) Infrastructurally, State Library is a Reference Library. Regional Libraries act as repositories and they lend books through branch libraries.

(v) The Director will be the overall charge of the department who should have decentralized control on libraries.

(vi) It has increased the range of library cess from 4 paise to 8 paise. The tax net for cess spreads on property tax, sales tax, vehicle tax and land revenue.

(vii) The State Council should provide for library and professional training for librarians.

3. Karnataka Public Libraries Act, 1965

The Karnataka Public Libraries Act of 1965 came into force with effect from April 22, 1965, when received the assent of the President of India. The main objective of the Act is "to provide for the establishment and maintenance of public libraries and the organization of a comprehensive rural and urban library service in the State."

The activities of the public libraries are guided and controlled by the education department. The State Librarian was the Head of the Department of Public Libraries. At present the Director of public libraries is heading the department.

The sailent features of this act are :

(i) It provides for a state-wide network of public libraries in the State of Karnataka.

(ii) State Library Authority is constituted to look after the governance of these libraries. It consists of 16 members including the President and Secretary. The Director of Public Libraries is the Secretary and the Minister for Education is the President.

(iii) A Department of Public Libraries is established as a full-fledged department of the State Government.

(iv) Like the other two Acts, the State Central Library serves as the apex body of the libraries.

(v) Local bodies have been established to govern library facilities.

(vi) The financial provision of the Act provides for the levy of a library cess in the form of a surcharge on the following taxes wherever they are levied:

  (a) Tax on land and buildings (Property tax);

  (b) Tax on entry of goods either for sale, use or consumption (Octroi);

  (e) Tax on vehicles; and

  (d) Tax on profession, trades, and employment.

The cess value can be increased from 3 paise to 6 paise per rupee with the sanction of the State Government.

Further, the State Government will provide an annual grant:

(a) to each Library Authority, excluding city Authorities, a sum equal to 3% of the land revenue collected in the concerned district;

(b) to the State Library Authority, this will be based on the Development Plan prepared by all the local bodies of the State; and

(e) the private libraries may be provided a grant based on request by the Director of Public Libraries.

The Act provides for a state-wide cadre for library and information personnel. They are all state government employees.

4. Maharashtra Public Libraries Act, 1967

This act was enacted in 1961. This is similar to the Karnataka Act. It established a Library Council and a separate Department of Libraries and also instituted the State Library Service. The salaries of those belonging to it are paid from the State Exchequer.

The Director of Public Libraries Plan, manage, organize, develop and maintain the public libraries in the state, except state central library. District level library committees have been set up for advising the government on all the matter concerning public libraries in the respective district.

The sailent features of the act are :

(i) The Maharashtra Act provides for financial grant by the State Government including the special grant. It also envisages grant from the Central Government, but, it does not provide for library cess as in the other three Acts. The general state grant is to be not less than 25 lakhs which is not inadequate to meet the needs of the entire state.

(ii) The Act also provides for appointment of qualified staff.

(iii) The Act provides far the establishment of libraries by each local body or any other voluntary organization. The department cannot be established straight away without the consent of local bodies.

(iv) The Act does not establish any State Central Library, but it proving for State Library Council.

(v) Like other Acts, the Maharashtra Act does not provide specialized units such as those for copyright deposit libraries, state bibliography centre etc,

(vi) The professional representation in the library authorities is weak. For example, the Secretary of the District Library Authority is the District Education Officer.

(vii) The Act provides for the appointment of qualified staff. However the professional library service has to be promoted by the state government.

5. West Bengal Public Libraries Act, 1979

West Bengal Government enacted the library legislation in 1979. Assent of the President of India was first published in the Calcutta Gazette, Extraordinary, of the 7th January, 1980. The aim of the Act is to provide for the establishment of public libraries in the state and to regulate, guide, control supervise and to grant recognition to the existing libraries in the state as also to provide for a comprehensive rural and urban library service in the state.

The sailent features of the act include :

(i) No provision for levying library cess.

(ii) The Director of the department is made fully responsible for the creation and maintenance of libraries in the state.

(iii) There is a state library council with the Minister of incharge of libraries as chairman and Director of library as secretary. It acts as an advisory body on all the matters connected with public libraries in the state.

(iv) Each revenue district can constitute a Local Library Authority for which the District Magistrate will be the chairman and District Library Officer as Secretary.

(v) Each district can appoint a District Library Officer.

(vi) The state central library shall receive the copy of the book published in the country under the provision made in the Press and Registration Act of 1867.

6. Manipur Public Libraries Act, 1988

A small State, Manipur, located in the eastern part of India got the opportunity for library legislation in 1988. The Salient features of the Manipur Public Libraries Act are given here under :

(i) No provision for levying library cess.

(ii) The provision has been made for the constitution of the state library committee, which is advisory in nature to advise the state government on all the matters related to public libraries in the state. The Minister incharge of education will be its Chairman and Director the ex-officio Secretary.

(iii) The provisions are also made in the act for the dissolution of the state library-committee, if its abuses the orders of the state government.

(iv) The provisions are also made in the act for the appointment of Director, who will be the incharge of the Dept. of Public libraries.

(v) The provision has been made in the act for the establishment of District Library and the constitutions of the District Library Authorities.

(vi) Finally, the Director of public libraries is made incharge of the department and to supervise the State Central Library the and District Libraries including all the branches in the State.

7. Kerala Public Libraries Act, 1989

Kerala Act is quite a different one, than the other Acts. But it is an unique one because of its democratic and more decentralised pattern. The characteristics of the Act are given below :

(i) There is a three tier administrative system for the organisation and administration of the public libraries system in the Kerala State. It comprises :

(a) Kerala State Library Council

(b) district Library Council

(c) Taluk Library Union

(ii) The provision has been made for the Collection of library cess and one percent of total education budget is reserved for the establishment and the maintenance of the public libraries in the state.

(iii) There is a provision in the act for the constitution of state library council and an executive committee. The state library council is autonomous in nature and is responsible for the creation and maintenance of department of public libraries and the libraries established in the state

(iv) The another unique feature of the Kerala act is the creation of state executive committee, there is a provision for electing its president and other office bearers among the members themselves. This is also advisable for the appointment of secretary for state library council.

(v) The provisions are made for the creation of District and Taluk council/s. These councils are given a power to distribute the grants within the district and taluk.

(vi) Library cess will be levied in the form of surcharge on building tax or property tax in the area with the jurisdiction of panchayats, municipalities and corporations.

(vii) The State Library Council shall maintain a fund called State Library Fund from which all the expenses of the State Library Council, District Library Councils and Taluk Library Unions shall be met. The library cess collected in the State and the grants of the State and Central Governments etc., will be credited to the State Library Fund only.

(viii) Reservation to at least one women and one person belonging to scheduled castes and scheduled tribes in all committees.

8. Haryana Public Libraries Act, 1989

The Haryana State was formed in the year 1966, carved out from the earlier Punjab State. Haryana Public Library Act was passed in 1989. Haryana Public Library Act has got the following features :

(i) Every local body in a district may levy in its area a library cess in the form of surcharge on property tax. The rate is fixed by the state government from time to time.

(ii) The provisions are made for the constitution and establishment of state library authority for which the Minister-in-charge is the Chairman and Director as Secretary which is advisory in nature. He can advise the state government on all the matters relating to public libraries.

(iii) The state government shall constitute a State Library Directorate which shall be the part of the government and is responsible for the establishment and maintenance of the libraries in the state.

(iv) The provision has been made for the establishment of the State Central Library under the incharge of the State Librarian. This is responsible for the selection, acquisition and the proper maintenance of reference books in the library

(v) The provisions are also made to constitute a district and city library committee. These committees are assigned to perform the specific functions mentioned in the act.

(vi) The provision has been made for the creation of Block and

Panchayat Library Committee and is very much similar to local library authorities in the Karnataka act.

(vii) The employees of the department are treated at par with the employees of the other government departments and specific qualifications and rules for the recruitment etc. are mentioned in the act.

(viii) The another important feature of this act is the creation of three types of public library funds viz., State, District and City or Town or Block or Village Library Fund.

9. Mizoram Public Libraries Act, 1993

Mizoram became a full fledged State in 1987. Within five years, it enacted the library Act in 1993. It possessed the following special features.

(i) No provision for levying library cess.

(ii) The provision is made for the constitution of state library council under the chairmanship of the Minister of Education and Human Resource Development. The state librarian shall be the ex-officio secretary of the council.

(iii) The council shall advise the government on all matters relating to libraries and also with regards to promotion and development of library services in the state.

(iv) The department of public libraries is constituted with a Director at its head and he is assisted by Deputy Directors, Joint Directors. Additional Directors etc.

(v) Under the provisions of the act, the following type of libraries are established :

- (a) State library;
- (b) District library;
- (c) Sub-Divisional library;
- (d) Village library.

(vi) There is a provision for financial assistance to recognised village libraries.

(vii) The another important salient feature of the act is that all the officers and other employees of the department are paid from the consolidated fund of the state.

10. Goa Public Library Act, 1994

This act was enacted in 1994. The salient features of this act are:

(i) The provision has been made to collect the library cess in the form of a surcharge on the excise duty payable under Goa Excise Duty Act 1964 at the rate of 50 paise per proof litre of the Indian Made Foreign Liquor (IMFL) and at the rate of 50 paise per bulk litre of beer.

(ii) There is a State Library Council with the Minister in-charge libraries as Chairman and the Director of Public Libraries as Secretary. The council shall advise the state library development cell in all technical matters relating to the library development and organization.

(iii) The provision has been made for the creation of the state library development cell which shall be a department of the government and this has been given the fullest responsibility including the distribution of grants to aided libraries.

(iv) The state central library has been established and it is also acting as a state reference library.

(v) The provisions are also made for the constitution of district taluk and village library committee to supervise the activities of the libraries in their jurisdiction.

(vi) The government has created a separate cadres for public library employees similar to those of the employees of other departments and laid down the qualifications, terms and conditions etc.

Concluding, it can be said that, to cater to the needs of the people of the country, library services are essential to achieve the developmental goals, improve the quality of life and preserve and make known the country's as well as the state's cultural heritage in its multiple forms. The public library service acts as intellectual catalyst for socio-economic development by providing facilities for the purpose of acquiring education and information as well as for recreation, aesthetic appreciation and research. Generally it is believed that where formal education ends, informal education begins and a lifelong learning process is continued with the support of free public library service.

Q. : Compare various provisions made out in any two library acts of India.

or

State the provision of finance for public services in Maharastra, Manipur and Goa or Goa vs. Mizoram public libraries act.

Ans. : There are following criteria for the purposes of a Library Acts.

(i) Public access to libraries,

(ii) Provision for financial management,

(iii) Human resources, and

(iv) Establishment of a governance system.

One by one comparison under each head is given here :

1. Public Access to Libraries

(i) Tamil Nadu

As per the Madras Act (1948), the government has provided for about 4,500 Public Libraries, 20 District Libraries, 7 Mobile libraries, 1538 Branch Libraries, 2,500 Village Libraries. They provide access to 24 lakhs volumes of documents. There were around 2 crores registered borrowers, and 5 crores visitors to libraries per annum. However, the volumes used can be categorised into those consulted, 2 crore; and borrowed 3 crore volumes. Borrowing of books is around 1 volume per literate person.

(ii) Andhra Pradesh

Andhra Pradesh has a total of about 4,000 public library nodes viz. one State Central Library, 6 Regional Libraries, 1426 Branch Libraries, 344 Village Libraries and 3 Mobile libraries under Zilla Granthalaya Sansthas and about 2,400 aided libraries. They provide access to about one crore volumes. They have registered borrowers of about 2 lakh persons, and about 2 crore visitors to consult books in libraries. The borrowing is about 1.5 volume per literate person.

(iii) Karnataka

Karnataka State has a structure of one State Central Library, 20 District Central Libraries (10 District Central Libraries are having library and the remaining 10 are having office only). There are 15 City Central

Libraries, 392 Branch Libraries, 1151 Mandal Libraries and 11 Mobile Libraries, with 6.54 lakh registered borrowers and a total book stock of 37 lakhs. About 8 lakh people visit the libraries in a year.

(iv) Maharashtra

Maharashtra, is the fifth state to have a library Act. It has around 5900 Public Library nodes. Of these, one is a State Central Library, 5 Divisional Libraries, 8 District Libraries, 31 District Public Libraries, 259 Taluk Libraries and 5589 other types of Libraries. They provide access to about 50 lakh of books. The number of registered borrowers is more than 60 thousands and consulting readers is around 60 lakhs per annum.

(v) West Bengal

West Bengal has about 3500 Public Library nodes. These include a State Library, 21 District Libraries, 234 Town Libraries, 2,300 Government sponsored Libraries and 200 other type of Libraries. There are additional District Libraries at Siliguri and City Central Library at Durgapur.

(vi) Manipur

This State has one State Central Library at Imphal and five District Libraries, and about one hundred Public Libraries are functioning which are managed by voluntary organizations.

(vii) Kerala

Public access is more in Kerala State, which now achieved cent per cent literacy through Total Literacy Campaign. The earlier Trivendrum Public Library was upgraded as State Central Library, after the formation of Kerala State. There are about 3030 libraries located at District. Taluk and village level accessible to the public.

(viii) Haryana

The District Library of Ambala, was upgraded as State Central Library of Haryana in 1967. 12 District Libraries were established in the State. In addition to it 11 libraries at Municipal areas, 11 sub-divisional libraries are working for the people.

(ix) Mizoram

After the formation of the State, State Library was established at Aizawl and two more District Libraries started functioning. There are three sub-divisional libraries accessible to the people. About 80 village libraries are also recognised by the State Planning committee.

(x) Goa

A small State, with the influence of Portuguese rule has a Central Library fora long time. Five taluk libraries and fifty six rural libraries are functioning at village level.

2. Financial Provision

The financial status of these library acts in different states is as under :

(i) Tamil Nadu

Tamil Nadu Public Libraries have three types of library; the State Central Library, Connemara Public Library and the Kaurmani Nilayan Library, a Government Oriental Manuscripts Library maintained by Government Funds. The District Central Libraries, and Branch Libraries established under the Act are maintained from Library Fund comprise of Library Cess and Government's matching contribution. Besides this, the government is giving grant-in-aid to the libraries such as, Thanjavur Saraswati Mahal Library maintained by local bodies and voluntary organisations.

(ii) Andhra Pradesh

The total expenditure on Government Libraries is borne by the Government. The establishment charges of Zilla Granthalaya Sanstha will be met by the Government. The Expenditure on other items such as books, periodicals, buildings etc., will be met from library fund of the City/Zilla Granthalaya Sansthas. They provide some grant-in-aid to private libraries.

(iii) Karnataka

The State Central Library is funded fully by the State Government. The libraries at District and City level, including Branch Libraries are financed from 'Library Fund'. Under the provision of this Act, Library cess is levied as surcharge on properties tax, motor vehicle tax and entertainment taxes. The Cess is collected by the local bodies such as, Municipal Corporations, Municipalities, District Boards and Village Panchayats. The State Government provides for the salaries of the staff of the public libraries at all levels.

(iv) Maharashtra

Maharashtra Act does not levy any library cess, however, the State Government has to provide for at atleast 25 lakh of rupees as grant-in-aid for library development. This does not include administrative and establishment expenditure. Five Divisional Libraries and eight District Libraries in Vidarbha are fully financed by the Government of Maharashtra.

(v) West Bengal

In West Bengal, since there is no provision for levying library cess, the entire expenditure on public libraries, started through the provisions of the Act, is to be met from the consolidated fund of the State. Every Local Library Authority shall maintain library fund out of the grant received from Government, contribution of gifts, income from endowments etc. However, a few private libraries will get grant in aid from the government, for their maintenance.

(vi) Manipur

In Manipur Act, as there is no provision for library cess, the State Government will meet the total expenditure from the State funds. This State will also support the private libraries with grant-in-aid.

(vii) Kerala

There is a provision for library cess in the Kerala Act. The State Government is helping the libraries by grant-in-aid, through the State Funds.

(viii) Haryana, (ix) Mizoram and (x) Goa

The same position prevails in Haryana as in the case of Kerala. The Library Act is yet to be implemented fully in these States.

3. Human Resources

The library staff in different states are provided variously as under :

(i) Tamil Nadu

The State has Directorate of Public Libraries which supervises, directs and runs public library service. There is a Librarian to manage the State Central Library i.e., Connemara Public Library. The District Central Library is manned by a trained librarian and the Branch Library is usually manned by a semi-trained person. The delivery stations are generally looked after by local elementary school teachers employee on part-time basis on monthly remuneration.

Each District Central Library is inspected by the Directorate of Public Libraries. Each Branch Library is inspected by the District Library Officer.

(ii) Andhra Pradesh

The Director of Public Libraries is the controlling officer for the library system in the state. All the libraries in the system are managed by professionals only. The Librarian, City/District Central Library is the Ex-officio Secretary of the City/Zilla Granthalaya Sanstha. The number of professionals are about 250 and semi-professionals are more than 1000 in number.

(iii) Karnataka

This state has a Director of Public Libraries to supervise and direct all matters relating to public libraries. The State, City, District and Branch Libraries are managed by professionals. The strength of the library staff in public libraries is around 500. The professional strength is around 150 with minimum qualification of degree in Library Science but several have MLISc degree. Besides, there are many certificate holders. There are also 300 non-professional and about 150 unskilled workers. The entire technical staff of the public libraries comes under the cadre of 'Karnataka Library Service'.

(iv) Maharashtra

Maharashtra Act provides for a Director of Libraries as the Head of the Department of Public Library Service. He is responsible for planning, maintenance and organization of public library service in the state. There is one Assistant Director in each of the 5 divisions to assist the Director. The libraries upto district and town level are maintained by professionals.

(v) West Bengal

West Bengal Act provides a post of a Director of Libraries, as Chief Executive of the public library system. The State Central Library, Calcutta Metropolitan Library, District Libraries and Town Libraries are managed by professional librarians.

(vi) Manipur

There is provision in the Act to appoint a Director of Public

Libraries. Presently, the Chief Librarian of the State Central Library, Imphal is looking after the matters in libraries. The total number of professionals working in Public libraries does not exceed 20 in the State.

(vii) Kerala

The special feature of the Kerala Act is that there is no post of Director of Public Libraries. Only after the full implementation of the act, the position of the staff will be clear.

(viii) Haryana

Since the Haryana Act has not come fully into force, the personnel who are managing public libraries are under the control of Director of Higher Education, Haryana. At present the state working in the State and District Libraries are treated as Government servants.

(ix) Mizoram

The Deputy Director of Education, Government of Mizoram, is the controlling officer. The State Library, District Library and Sub-Divisional Libraries are managed by the qualified Librarians which are not more than 20 in number.

(x) Goa

Central Libraries, Government of Goa. Panaji is the controlling officer of the human resource. In Goa about 25 professionals are working in State Central Library (Bibliotheca National De Nova Goa, and its five Taluk Libraries). Teacher Librarians are incharge of most of the Government village libraries.

4. Governance

(i) Tamil Nadu

The State Tamil Nadu comprises of Madras City and 23 Revenue Districts. There is a Local Library Authority - one for each Revenue District. From 1972, the Department of Public Libraries became the full fledged Department. The Director of Public Libraries is responsible for superintending and controlling the work of all local library authority constituted under Act. Till 1977, the District Educational Officers had acted as Ex-officio Secretaries of the Local Library Authorities. As per the recommendation of the Subbarayan Committee, the District Educational Officers of each Local Library Authority is rendering free library service to public by opening District Central Library at District

Head-Quarters, a Branch Library in one town, and library vans for some small villages and hamlets.

(ii) Andhra Pradesh

To organize and promote library service in the state, the Government of Andhra Pradesh amended the Act in 1989, and constituted Andhra Pradesh Granthalaya Parishad, an appex body.

The Parishad is the principal policy making body and exercises the powers and performs the functions as per the directions of the Government. The State has been divided into 23 Revenue Districts including the City of Hyderabad for the purpose of administering the library system. There is a Zilla Granthalaya Sanstha for each district and one City Granthalaya Sanstha for the Hyderabad City.

In the Pyramidal system of organization, the State Central Library is at the appex, the village library at the bottom and the Branch Libraries, District Central Libraries, and Regional Libraries in between them.

(iii) Karnataka

This State is divided into 20 revenue districts. A separate Department of Public Libraries started functioning with effect from 1 November 1966 as per the provisions of the Karnataka Public Libraries Act 1965. The department is responsible for the establishment and maintenance of public libraries and the organization of a comprehensive rural and urban libraries' service in the state. The Act provides for the establishment of the following libraries including Branch Libraries and Book Delivery Stations at :

(a) A State Central Library at Bangalore which will act as the reservoir of books for the entire state.

(b) A City Central Library for each of the 15 principal cities.

(c) A District Central Library for each of the 20 Revenue Districts in the State.

In the state, three library authorities have been established; the Karnataka State Library Authority which advises the State Government on matters related to library development in the state, and acts as managing authority for the State Central Library; the Local Library Authorities of the major cities and the Revenue Districts which will look after the matters of public libraries in their respective jurisdiction.

There is a fair amount of democratic representation as well as technical expertise built into the composition of the State Library Authority.

(iv) Maharashtra

In Maharashtra, the State Library Council has been set up to advise the Government on all matters concerning libraries, which comprises of 28 members with the Minister of Education as the Ex-officio Chairman, and the Director of Libraries as the Ex-officio Member Secretary. At District Level, District Library Committees have been set up for advising the government on all matters concerning public libraries in their respective areas. The Directorate of public libraries with a Director as its head looks after the planning, management, organization, development and maintenance of public libraries and the library system in the state. This state has 35 revenue Districts.

(v) West Bengal

This state has 17 Revenue Districts. The Act provides for the creation of a State Library Council and Local Library Authorities. Under the control of Director of Libraries, the Public Library System, with State Central Library at the appex, Calcutta Metropolitan Library, District Libraries, Town Libraries and Rural Libraries will function with a paramedical structure and governance.

(vi) Manipur

Manipur has 8 Revenue Districts. The State, Central Library, Imphal is managed by Education Department and the District Libraries are attached to District Educational Officers.

(vii) Kerala

This state is divided into 14 Districts. Trivandrum Public Library is the only Public Library directly managed by State Government. The Municipal Libraries and the Panchyat Libraries are managed by the Concerned local bodies.

(viii) Haryana

The State haryana was formed in the year 1966 with 17 revenue Districts. Haryana Library Administration is still under the control of Department of Higher Education.

Chart showing comparison of Libraries Acts in Different States

State	Year	Total Number of Libraries	Levels of Libraries	Cess	State grant
1. Tamilnadu	1948	4000	One State Central library, six Regional libraries, 1426 Branch libraries, 4 Mobile libraries, 344 Villages libraries, 1400 other libraries.	Library cess on property tax or house tax	A matching grant not less than the cess collected
2. Andhra Pradesh	1960	4000	One state Central Library 15 City Central library, 20 District Central libraries, 329 Branch libraries, 10 Grant-in-aid libraries, 2140 other libraries.	Library cess on House tax and properties	Payment of staff salaries
3. Karnataka	1965	2700	One State Central library, 5 Division libraries, 8 District libraries, 31 District Public libraries, 259 Taluka libraries, 5589 other libraries	Library cess on lands and buildings, octroi, duty, vehicle tax, taxes on professions.	Grant-in-aid from government for payment of staff salaries.

State		Year	Total Number of Libraries	Levels of Libraries	Cess	State grant
4.	Maharastra	1967	5900	One state Central library, 20 District libraries, 1538 Branch libraries, 7 Mobile libraries, 2500 village libraries.	No library cess	State Grant
5.	West Bengal	1979	4000	One State central library, 6 Regional libraries, 1629 libraries under zilla Parishad, 2400 aided libraries.	No library cess	State Grant
6.	Manipur	1988	106	One State Central Library One District libraries-5 Public libraries-100	No library cess	State Grant
7.	Kerala	1989	3030	State Central library District libraries, Taluka libraries, Village libraries.	Library cess on buildings or property tax	Grant-in-aid from government

State	Year	Total Number of Libraries	Levels of Libraries	Cess	State grant
8. Haryana	1989	36	State District Municipal Libraries, Sub-divisional libraries	Library cess on property tax and house tax	Grant-in-aid from government
9. Mizoram	1993	86	State library District library Sub-divisional libraries Villages libraries	No library cess	State Grant
10. Goa	1994	62	Central library- 1 Tuluka library- 5 Rural libraries-56	No library cess	State Grant

(ix) Mizoram

Mizoram is a small state with 3 Revenue Districts. In Mizoram, Deputy Director of Education is made for controlling the Public Libraries.

(x) Goa

Goa is the smallest state with two Revenue Districts. In Goa, the Curator, Central Library Government of Goa is looking after the Public Libraries.

Recently, Gujarat Public Libraries Act (2001) and Orissa Public Libraries Act have also been introduced and their working is in progress.

Q. : Write a brief note on a Model Library Act.

or

Discuss the sailent features and structure of Model Library Act.

Ans. : Model Library Act is a legislation for setting up a network of libraries. It should consists of following :

Preamble

Whereas it is expedient to provide for the establishment and maintenance of a system of Public Libraries and for the comprehensive development and organization of city, rural and other kinds of library service in the State.

Sailent Features of Model Library Act

(i) It should define all the basic concepts or instruments or components for a library service system.

(ii) It should define the configurational structure of the system of libraries.

(iii) It should state the governance apparatus, such as Library Committee, Board of Management and the like.

(iv) It should define the system of cadre, recruitment, and concept of professional excellence of library and information professionals.

(v) It should set up tiers of organization for continuous financial support and utilization.

(vi) It should provide for different types of service to regular and specialized citizens.

(vii) It should set up the *ways of reporting services* to the professional activities as well as administrative authorities. It should also help to monitor the system.

(viii) It should provide for a complete library system that would look into preservation of various types of documents as well as dissemination of information contained in them.

(ix) The model act should link the state library system with other professional services system such as judicial, medical, research, educational, agricultural, industrial, administrative and defence systems.

Structure of Model Library Act

Some of the informational headings should contain, are as follows :

(i) Preliminaries

This part of the Act has to tell about the exact title and short title of the act. It should also include the definitions of concepts for understanding and interpretation.

(ii) State Library Authorities

This part of the Act covers the organizational systems and services. It delineates the authoritative linkages with the democratic system of the state. It should define the governance procedures and identify the officers of the system. It should define the constitution, membership, and functions of a variety of library committees including powers and limitations of the committee and principal officers.

(iii) The System of Network Libraries

It covers the constitution, formation, service and funding aspects of State Library, District Libraries, City Libraries and Rural Libraries, such as Village Libraries, etc.

(iv) State Central Library System

It defines the varieties of libraries for special purposes and services such as the State Library for Blind, State Library for Copyright Documents, etc.

(v) Financial Clauses

The methods of state funding, tax structure and collection of funds and their distribution and utilization, are to be spelt out to ensure a regular flow of funds and their deployment.

(vi) Manpower Structure

The type of professionals to be involved in the management of library have to be spelled out to ensure quality library service.

(vii) Rules

Rules for maintaining and controlling offences in Library usage must be framed for providing equal facilities to all.

7
Resource Sharing and Resource-Sharing Networks

Q. : What do you understand by library co-operation? Specify various areas of library co-operation.

or

Discuss the various forms of resource sharing.

or

What are the areas of resource sharing? Discuss them.

or

Examine the concept of resource sharing. Discuss the areas where this concept could be applied.

or

Resource sharing among the libraries eliminates duplication of money, manpower and material. Elucidate the statement.

Ans. : The co-operation may be defined as association of people or agencies in activities with common goals or objectives and with the purpose of providing specific benefits for all. The basic concept is that the benefits derived are shared by all. Library cooperation signifies a symbol of good will, an intent to share resources, knowledge, bibliographical data, facilities and other fruits of technology, man's ingenuity, and the result of accumulated wealth of knowledge.

The term "resource" applies to any thing, person, or action to which one turns for aid in time of need. The word "sharing" connotes apportioning, allowing, or contributing something that is owned, to benefit others. 'Resource sharing' in its most positive aspects entails reciprocity, implying a partnership in which each member has something useful to contribute to others and which one is willing and able to make available when needed.

By library resources, we mean the library materials, functions and services (Fig. 1). Library materials are of two types documentary and non-documentary. Documentary materials are those which are in the form of documents that include books, periodicals, reports, patents, standards, theses, and so on. Non-documentary materials include audio-visual aids, microforms, machine readable databases, computers, etc. The term functions connote acquisition, processing, storing, retrieving, maintenance, etc. 'Services' mean the activities which a library offers to its users and include, among others, lending of documents, reference service, documentation service, reprography service, etc. Expertise and experience of professional staff are also considered resources. Taken together, we can say that material persons, money of a library including its functions and services constitute its resources.

Library Resources

- **Personnel**
  - Experience
  - Expertise
- **Materials**
  - Books
  - Periodicals
  - Patents
  - Audio-Visual Aids
  - Equipment
- **Functions**
  - Acquisition
  - Processing
  - Storage
  - Retrieval
  - Maintenance
- **Services**
  - Lending
  - Reference
  - Documentation
  - Reprography
  - Translation

Fig. 1. Library Resources and their Breakdown

By sharing we mean sharing the use of material either by inter-library loan or by allowing users of one library to use material of another library. The functions can also be shared through cooperative acquisition, processing, retrieval, etc. Similarly services and expertise of one library can be shared with another. Equipment can also be shared. Computers, microfilm reader-printers, etc are costly equipment. So, it is not possible for all libraries to procure them. If a library possesses such equipment, other libraries can use them on time sharing basis.

Thus, library cooperation or resource sharing denotes a mode of operation whereby library functions are shared in common by a number of libraries. The objectives are to provide a positive effect :

— on the library user in terms of access to more materials or services, and/or

— on the library budget in terms of providing level service at less cost, increased service at level cost, or much more service at less cost than if undertaken individually.

— on opportunity for the collaborating libraries to increase their resources to provide better services and more facilities to the users without corresponding proportionate increase in expenditures. All libraries cooperating in such a scheme are merged as it were into a single unit with vast pool of resources. It is the transmigration of the individualistic philosophy of library service into a cooperation service.

Need of Resource Sharing or Library Cooperation

(i) Dr. Ranganathan first law of Library Science, "Books are for use" explains that it is the duty of the Librarian that he puts his collection to maximum use not only for the users visiting his library but also users scattered over other libraries. In order to satisfy the import of first law, library collections are for inter-library cooperation as well.

(ii) In modern times, self sufficiency remains only imaginative because of insufficient financial resources and explosion of literature in the form of ever increasing volumes of journals, current and back volumes, technical reports, conference papers, books and monographs, thesis and dissertations, patents, standards etc., hence inter-library cooperation is the need of the modern times.

(iii) 'Every reader his/her book' and 'Every book its reader' require special care and attention. The user must get his/her reading materials whether it is available with the library where he/she is registered or in any other library. Similarly every book demand its user. In both the cases inter-library cooperation, to satisfy user demand and the demand of the book that, "do not make me idle" require strengthening.

(iv) User's have different tastes of reading and study and different desires. These tend to change with time. Besides, new branches of knowledge and new technologies are also coming up. These also increases the user need and their demands. Therefore, libraries requires to provide extensive cooperation services to meet the needs of the users.

To overcome the problem of language barrier inter-library cooperation or resource sharing is an essential activity for the modern library to maximise library use with minimum resources.

(v) As we know, Library is a growing organism, thus, the collection of library is tend to increase every year by procurement of new documents. This leads to problem of storage of books. Nowadays, equipment like photocopies and personal computers are becoming quite common in libraries. These medium also occupy some space of the library. Starting of a new service also entails recruitment of staff and procurement equipment and stationery, which again consume space. All these make the space problem of a library acute particularly with reference to upkeep and maintenance. Thus, shortage of space too with the help of library cooperation or resource sharing can be solved to some extent.

(vi) If there is a scarcity of staff, we can use cooperative cataloguing or centralized cataloguing or classification of documents. Thus, the staff efforts can be scared by using such library cooperative activities.

Besides in modern ages, users demand are multi-disciplinary and these can be meet out with the help of micro-documents or computerized services. Such demands extensively require library cooperation or resource sharing at national and international level.

Forms of Resource Sharing

The following are the forms of resource sharing, where this concept can be applied.

(i) Acquisition

Libraries acquire books, periodicals, and other materials from publishers, booksellers etc. situated in and outside the country. Acquisition, apart from document selection involves placing orders, reminding the suppliers, passing of bills and a few other activities.

Procurement of foreign periodicals in India poses problems as subscriptions are to be paid in foreign currency. Release of foreign currency from banks is not only troublesome but also time-consuming. Some libraries place orders with some periodical subscription agencies within the country or abroad to avoid problems of foreign currency. Subscribing through these agencies is also not free from problems. Sometimes, these agencies place orders for periodicals very late, as a result of which, libraries either receive the first new issues quite late or do not receive them at all. Foreign publishers receiving the subscriptions late, in many cases fail to supply the first few issues for the year, which also go out of print. It is also seen that in many cases, these agencies do not place order for some titles at all. In such a situation, not only the library does not get the issues of the periodical, but also faces a problem in getting back the money from the agency.

All these activities can be reduced greatly through cooperative acquisition of documents. Moreover, it may bring down cost, earn larger discount and save time and the labour of individual libraries.

(ii) Cooperative and Centralized Cataloguing

Cooperative cataloguing is a part of union catalogue. The benefit of Cooperative Cataloguing will be uniformity in cataloguing and in classification and there will be uniformity in standardization, which will save the time for classification, cataloguing and standardization. Cooperative cataloguing and classification is done only for the benefit of the participating libraries.

Centralized cataloguing and classification is done by some central agency at one central place and the benefit goes to all the libraries. In this method, cataloguing is done by the central agency or by the publisher itself. They provide the catalogue card along with the document.

With the advent of computer networking, this task has become much easier. In the network, the data of all the books or documents catalogued by the libraries within the network are inputted through the terminals to the main-frame computer. Whether or not, a book has already been catalogued can be found out using the terminal of any library within the network. Suppose a library has to catalogue 30 books. The cataloguer finds out using the terminal whether any of the books he is going to catalogue has already been catalogued by some other library. The cataloguer may find that 16 books out of 30 he is intending to catalogue, have already been catalogued by some libraries within the network. So, he is to catalogue only 14 books which are not yet catalogued. The cataloguer just down-load the entries using the keyboard. The entries are monitored at the main library and modification or correction of the entries, if necessary, are done there, and finally entries are stored in the memory of the computer. The cataloguer informs main library to send the cards of all the 30 books that had to be catalogued. Main library sends the cards and the library does the rest of the job.

This is how the job of cataloguing is shared by all the libraries within the network, but the libraries forming pay of the network must follow the same cataloguing code, and the cataloguing code should meet the requirements of computerization.

Printed catalogue card service is another form of shared cataloguing. Some libraries, usually of national status, undertake this responsibility of producing printed catalogue cards which are available on a payment basis. In the United States, the Library of Congress, in United Kingdom, BNB and in the Soviet Union (now Russia), the All Union Book Chamber provide printed catalogue card service. The All Union Chamber provides, apart from bibliographical details, abstract books also in cards.

Another programme Cataloguing-in-Publication, a new programme is introduced by the Library of Congress. In this programme, the cataloguing data are printed usually on the reverse of the title page; author, title, series statement, note, subject and added entries, LC classification number, DDC classification number, LC card number and the ISBN. The data are given in the LC card format.

These data may useful to all cataloguers irrespective of the cataloguing rules they follow.

(iii) Cooperative Storage

Most of our libraries suffer from the chronic problem of space. The possessive mentality of libraries and the cumbersome procedure of weeding out of books, result in the piling up of old and less used materials in the library. As a result, at times, new acquisitions find their place on the floors rather than on shelves, or shelves become too jampacked for easy retrieval. Moreover, the maintenance and upkeep of the unused or little used collection not only consumes valuable space of the library, but also costs money and labour. Needless to say, they hinder the effective use of the library. For the purpose, cooperative storage is the best solution. The motive behind cooperative storage are:

(a) the assumption that libraries run out of space and relief must be obtained.

(b) the assumption that all libraries contain a great deal of material i.e., not being used very much.

So it is advantageous and logical to store little used and rare material at a common space built at low cost, located on cheap land, and less cost for maintenance and storage. It will also reduce duplication for reading material and provide free space in existing libraries.

(iv) Sharing of Equipments

Nowadays, libraries use different types of equipments for carrying out various jobs The most widely used ones are computers and reprographic equipments. The cost of personal computers has come down considerably and university libraries, libraries of big organisations or even smaller libraries can afford these machines. Quite a number of functions can be automated using personal computers.

For major automation in libraries, main-frame computers are necessary, which hardly any Indian library can afford. In such a situation, a number of libraries can cooperate-to procure a main-frame computer, and can use it on a time-sharing basis

Besides, many libraries do have palm-leaves manuscripts, numbering tens of thousands. Many others have 18th or 19th century printed documents, requiring conversion to microform for preservation. Developing good reprographic facility is, however, beyond the reach of most of the libraries. The only alternative is to develop such facilities on a cooperative basis.

(v) Inter-Library Loan

Inter-Library Loan is the most common and age-old form of resource sharing, prevalent among most of the libraries in the world. In this, a library gets a book or any other document from another library on loan for a certain period. The transaction takes place only between libraries. ILL or inter-library activity certainly saves the time of the users to get his/her information and document. Due to financial constraints, no library can possess or purchase all the documents published. Thus, one has to depend upon others collection.

In our country inter-library loan transactions are operating reasonably well, though it could be still better.

There is no national policy which binds libraries to take part in such cooperative activities. The practice of inter-library loan is confined mainly to cities because the document can be easily located, obtained and returned speedily and at lesser cost. Postal rates in India being quite high, getting or sending a document by post, at times becomes costlier than the document itself. Moreover, documents sometimes get lost in postal transit. Hence inter-library loan by post is usually avoided. However, for obtaining documents from far-flung cities, postal channel is obviously better than others.

Problems of Resource Sharing

The following are some of the major problems in the field of resource sharing.

(i) The lack of public knowledge about the location and usage of available resources as well as the benefits thereof.

(ii) It is hard to establish national standards.

(iii) The sharing of resources is no remedy when resources are generally inadequate at the local level.

(iv) Local libraries do not have the necessary staff expertize to handle the services and products of new technology.

(v) Copyright has affected the continuing development of cooperative programmes and networks among libraries.

(vi) Cooperative/coordinated acquisitions programmes are difficult to carry out because they tend to infringe upon prerogatives of member libraries.

(vii) Bibliographic and performance standards (e.g., the MARC format and AACR-2) must be identified and agreed upon before a national networking scheme can become operational.

(viii) At a time when funds at almost every level are not available to support on current costs, it is hard to promote library cooperation and resource sharing.

(ix) Costs relating to networks are still not being considered by local bodies as a part of the library's normal operating budget. Hence, a large scale resource sharing programme would be considerably difficult.

(x) Library systems add an additional complication to the need to locate shared but widely scattered materials.

(xi) A union card catalogue of members holding becomes formidably costly when the size of the files to be maintained is projected into the future.

(xii) As libraries vary in types of objectives, functions and source of funds, the success of resource sharing remains doubtful.

Conditions for Success of Resource Sharing

As we know, Resource sharing is based on willingness to work together to achieve mutual benefit, each participant is responsible towards its share for the attainment of the goal. Some of the conditions for better sharing are :-

(i) Library Legislation or Government Sanctions both at national and international level, state level, providing clauses for sharing resources including ILL, exchange of publication at various levels, as well as provision of finance is essential.

(ii) Matters relating to reduce sharing should be discussed periodically at the AIU, UGC and VC's conferences etc.

(iii) To reduce the operational work load, ILL forms should be designed and standardized by the participating libraries.

(iv) Adequate reprographic facilities should be provided extensively at all libraries to facilitate the resource sharing.

(v) Microfilms and photocopies of documents should be made available at nominal charges in all libraries.

(vi) Union catalogue of holding of a locality, region, state level libraries should be prepared and maintained.

(vii) Concessional postal/ communication charges be taken for the resources sharing services.

(viii) The policy of specialization of libraries in certain subject fields on the line of 'Farmington Plan" of USA will facilitate resource sharing.

Tremendous technological change has affected the every field of world, so is the case with libraries, needs of researches and library systems. Multiplier users, remote access and round the clock availability of information, resource sharing, multi-dimensional services are possible through the information and computer network at local, national and international level. Suitable human resources for library automation is also very essential. It is advisable to include exchange programmes opportunities as an integral part of the educational programme for the libraries and administrations. Besides, for effective application of any technology, well-trained and capable professional staff should also be exchanged to create environment.

Criticism of Resource Sharing

Resource sharing despite its numerous plus points, has certain minus points too, critics voice concern of the following points;

(i) If all libraries turn to resource sharing, no library will have books to lend.

(ii) If resource sharing fails many libraries will not be able to fill up the gaps afterwards.

(iii) A high level of service, might not be attained by resource sharing with the limited technology and organizational structure, particularly in India.

(iv) The cost that may be incurred for obtaining a book through resource sharing may equal or even exceed the cost of the book itself.

(v) Resource sharing is likely to adversely affect the publishing industry, which may lead to a big hike in prices of books and this hike may completely offset the gains of resource sharing.

(vi) The rich libraries may have to share a bigger burden and act more as a lender rather than a borrower, which may not be beneficial to them.

But inspite of above some drawbacks, resource sharing concept is flourished well and it is doing its own jobs and serving for the best of users.

Q. : What do you mean by networking? Define aims and objectives of library networks. Also discuss some of the library networks working for resource sharing in brief.

Ans. : A Network can be defined as a group of individuals or organizations that are interconnected. The advent of computers and new developments in telecommunication technology made networking a global phenomenon. Library and information institutions are forming networks to achieve better resource sharing and to provide better service to its users. These networks help in :

(i) On-line retrieval of bibliographic, numeric, as well as full-text databases;

(ii) Compilation of reading lists, topical bibliographies, etc.;

(iii) To have bibliographic control by integrating national library catalogues, etc.;

(iv) Automatic book requesting systems;

(v) Use of CD-ROM products and services;

(vi) Remote data entry facility;

(vii) Downloading of information;

(viii) Library mailing, inter-library requests and lending etc.;

(ix) Document delivery; and

(x) Access to public domine information/data/software etc.

Aims and Objectives of Library Networks

Some of aims and objectives of the library networks are :

(i) To promote sharing of resources;

(ii) Assist in acquisition and processing of material;

(iii) Exchange of documents and data;

(iv) Cooperation and coordination in collection development;

(v) Help in the establishment of referral service, on-line retrieval of information and on-line union catalogues;

(vi) To build bibliographic databases;

(vii) To build various other databases like that of projects, specialists, institutions, etc;

(viii) Electronic Mailing;

(ix) File transferring;

(x) Evolving standards and guidelines in techniques, methods, procedures, hardware, software, services and so on.

Important Library Networks

The need for networking of libraries with the objective of resource sharing was felt in the 1980s after witnessing a great deal of progress made by the developed countries in this direction. The 'Working Group' of the Planning Commission on libraries and informatics headed by Dr. N, Seshagiri recommended the need for modernization of library services and inter-linking of library systems during the 7th plan period (1985-1990).

In 1985, NISSAT convened a meeting under the chairmanship of Director-General, CSIR. One of the recommendations of this meeting was establishment of a Science and Technology Library in Calcutta and the promotion of automation and networking in the city. CMC Ltd. was commissioned by NISSAT to prepare the feasibility report on the Calcutta Library Network (CALIBNET). The report was completed and published in 1989. In the meanwhile, in January 1988, India International Centre, New Delhi with the support of NISSAT began the work on Delhi Library Network (DELNET) as a project of the Centre. In July 1992, it was registered as a society under the Societies Registration Act of 1860.

The recommendations of the Working Group on Modernization of Library Service and Informatics headed by Dr. Seshagiri, paved the way for the establishment of an Information and Library Network (INFLIBNET). The report of INFLIBNET was published in 1989. In 1991, INFLIBNET opened its office at Ahmedabad as soon as funds became available under the Eighth Plan, INFLIBNET began its work. There are many other networks were also developed during recent years, such as NICNET, INDONET, I-NET, ERNET, BINET, SAILNET, BANKNET, DESINET, BHELNET, RAIL-NET, SIRNET, OILCOMNET, GAILNE ONGCNET. MALIBNET, PISNENET and BONET etc. But these have not made much progress as the CALIBNET, DELNET and the INFLIBNET did.

A brief discussion on CALIBNET, DELNET and INFLIBNET is made here :

1. CALIBNET : CALIBNET stands for Calcutta Library Networks. It was sponsored by NISSAT which initiated the action for the preparation of a feasibility report by CMC. According to the feasibility report, CALIBNET was to be a network of 40 libraries. It was to be developed in two phases. NISSAT provided funds for the development of software package (MAITRAYEE) based on INGRESS 502 for CALIBNET. This package was developed by CMC Ltd.

Details regarding the total quantity of machine-readable data produced by different participating libraries using MAITRAYEE package of software are not readily available. CALIBNET is providing access to INTERNET and is offering CD-ROM database searching facility. Whether CALIBNET has started the creation of a union catalogue for the books available in the participating libraries is not known.

It appears that CALIBNET has not yet developed itself into a resource sharing network of libraries in Calcutta as was envisaged. A full picture of CALIBNET and the value-added products it has developed so far to aid the resource sharing activity by libraries in Calcutta has yet to emerge.

2. DELNET : It was originally started as a project of India International Centre (IIC) New Delhi, with the financial support from NISSAT. The financial support continued for the period 1988 to 1992. It became a registered society in March 1992. Some of the salient features of the network are:

(i) It has 67 institutional libraries as its members and the membership is on the increase from year to year.

(ii) In order to promote resource sharing among member libraries DELNET has, so far, created the following:

- (a) Union catalogue of books available in the member libraries in computer-readable form.
- (b) Union list of periodicals.
  - (i) Union list of scientific and technical periodicals;
  - (ii) Union list of social science periodicals;
  - (iii) Union list of periodicals in humanities.
- (c) Specialists database.
- (d) Database of articles.
- (e) Union catalogue of periodicals.
- (i) Database of language publications.

(iii) DELSIS, the networking software based on BASIS plus which can accommodate and retrieve millions of bibliographic and full text records was developed by DELNET itself.

(iv) INTERNET access and E-mail facilities are provided for its members. DELNET has also created a Home Page on WWW, which can be accessed on INTERNET at the following address: http://www.nic or http://www.nic in/delnet;

(v) It is claimed by DELNET that it has saved nearly Rs. 1 crore on the part of participating libraries through rationalisation of foreign periodicals in the field of physical sciences, medical sciences and agricultural sciences.

(vi) DELNET has been arranging training programmes for the staff members of the participating libraries and providing them an exposure to the application of modern technology.

It may stated that DELNET has made a break through in resource sharing activities and has thus become the first operational library network in India. It is on the path of enlarging its activities and is contemplating to develop an on-line database of 'Books in Print: New Titles', with the cooperation of some renowned publishers.

3. INFLIBNET : The INFLIBNET programme was conceptualised by the then Chairman of UGC Prof. Yash Pal. As a result of UGC's efforts to help the university libraries to share their resources and to avoid the duplication of holdings, INFLIBNET was established in the year 1988, with objectives set forth as :

— to evolve a national network, interconnecting various libraries and information centres in the country and to improve the capability in information handling and service;

— to provide access to document collection of libraries by creating on-line union catalogue of monographs, serials, and non-book materials;

— to provide improved access to bibliographic numerical and factorial databases with particular emphasis on those databases created indigenously by the Sectorial Information Centres of NISSAT and UGC Information centres;

— to establish gatways for on-line accessing of information;

— to provide document delivery service by enriching information sources of libraries having rich collection in specific areas;

— to optimize information resource utilization through resource sharing;

— to implement computerization of operations and services in libraries and information centres following uniform standards;

— to facilitate scientific communication among scientists, technologists, researchers, social scientists, academics, faculties and students through electronic mail, bulletin board, file transfer, computer/audio/video conferencing, etc.;

— to enable users disbursed all over the country to have access to information regarding books, monographs, serials, and non-book materials by locating the sources where available, and to obtain them through the facilities of new technologies and union catalogue of documents;

— to encourage cooperation among libraries, documentation centres, information centres in the country, so that the resources can be pooled for the benefit of weaker resource centres by the stronger ones;

— to develop suitable professional manpower of appropriate quality to establish and manage and sustain the INFLIBNET and;

— to evolve standards and uniform guidelines in techniques, methods, procedures, hardware and software and services and so on, and promote adoption in actual practice by all libraries in order to facilitate exchange of resources towards optimization.

Services of INFLIBNET

INFLIBNET is planned and designed as a multiple function/ service network. It is providing the following services:

(i) Catalogue based service

(ii) Database services

(iii) Document supply service

(iv) Collection development (helping different participants in acquisition and procurement)

(v) Communication based services

(i) Catalogue Based Services : Catalogue services comprise of shared cataloguing of monographs, serials and non-book materials, compilation of union catalogue of books, serials and non-book materials, provision of on-line access for shared cataloguing and location identification, assisting in catalogue production in card, book, magnetic tape/floppy, etc.

(ii) Data Base Services : These include searching of databases for current as well as retrospective services, provision of computer-based SDI and provision of non-bibliographic information such as on-going and completed projects, institutions and specialist by compiling, maintaining and searching such non-bibliographic databases.

(iii) Document Supply Services : It include inter-library loan service and document delivery service through fax/non-fax and Internet etc.

(iv) Collection Development Service : It is basically intended to help the member libraries in selection, acquisition and procurement aspects.

(v) Communication Based Services : These services include :

— Referral services

— Electronic-mail service

— Bulletin Board - view/update bulletin board

— Academic communication through electronic mail, file transfer, computer/audio/video conferencing, etc.

Achievements of INFLIBNET

(i) It regularly arrange training programmes for participating universities to train their man power in the field of automation.

(ii) It has brought out following publication by now.

(a) Compilation of a union catalogue

(b) Databases of thesis/dissertations and

(c) Serials database

(iii) It prepare guidelines for data capturing, encouraging library automation activities, developments of suitable software and implementing at participating libraries.

(iv) It has also developed its own library software named SOUL for library automation.

(v) It arranges annual conference CALIBER to discuss recent developments in the field of library and information science at a common platform.

By now 10 such conferences have been arranged including 2 international ones.

(vi) It also arranges IRTPLA, training programmes at local level to train the man power in regional languages at selected spots.

Besides, recently it is working as a media agency to implement UGC-INFONET programme of University Grants Commission which is started in the December 2003. Through this programme, free access of e-journals will be provided to each and every participating university through INTERNET connectivity. In a few universities, this facility has already been provided and they are getting benefits of e-access. Rest of the universities are at developing stage.

8
User Education and User Studies

Q. : Distinguish user studies and user education. What are the different methods of user studies?

or

Explain the different types of methodologies associated with user studies.

or

Discuss the role of information technology in promoting user education.

Ans. : Libraries being the service centres, help the users to get the information they want. For this purpose, the library staff has developed a number of tools and techniques. The classified arrangement of books on the shelves helps the users to locate easily, the books they want. The library catalogue helps to locate the book on the shelf. The various maps, plans, guides, etc. provided in the library helps the users to find their way in the complex library mechanism. In addition, the Reference Library Staff provides personalised service whenever the user is in difficulty. The lending service, reference service, bibliographic, inter-library loan, translation service and reprography etc. are the general services provided by the library.

But a new user sometime finds himself in trouble to use the available resources. Hence, to help the users to better utilize the library services, some programmes are arranged to make aware them about the services and handling of library resources. Such programmes fall under the preview of user education. Sometimes, user education programmers are also known as internal extension services.

User Education Prgrammes

For helping the users in using library resources, reference service is given at personalized level. But, apart from providing assistance to users the reference librarians or reference assistants are expected to orient the users in the library mechanism, because libraries are these days mechanised things. Mechanised things are dependent ones. One needs orientation to exploit the resources to their fullest extent. The activities to be carried out by the reference staff within the library to orient or educate the users are called 'User Education Activities' or 'Internal Extension Activities. Such 'user education' or 'orientation' programme not only help the users in exploiting the resources of a library, but also, help the library staff in better organization and management of the libraries. Some of these programmes discussed below:

(i) Orientation into the Library Mechanism : The reference staff may orient the users either formally or informally into the library systems. In an informal way, the user may be taken to the Library Map/ Plan and explain the various sections, special collections and services. The reference staff may take the user personally to various sections and explain the type of material available, kind of information one can get, etc. It will be more effective if it is demonstrated to the user as to how to locate the information from various types of source material. In the formal system of orientation, the structured orientation programme may be planned wherein one can combine lectures supported by audio-visual aids; tour around the library demonstration etc., can be used effectively.

(ii) Formal Programmes : In the formal programmes, the following areas may be comprehended:

(a) **Introduction to the Library :** Concept and role of the library; types of libraries; kinds of documents; sections of a library; services provided, etc.

(b) **Documents :** Sources-Primary, Secondary and Tertiary, Kinds-Books, Periodicals, Audio-Visual, etc.

(c) **Parts of a Book :** Preliminaries- Half title page, Title page, Back of the title page, Table of contents, Preface, Introduction, Body of the Book-parts, Chapters, Paragraphs, Sectional headings, References, Notes, etc., End matter - Notes, References, Index etc.

(d) **Care of Books :** How to pick-up a book from the shelf, opening of the book for consultation, protecting books from its enemies, improper ways of handling, etc.

(e) **Arrangement of Material :** Books-textbooks, reference books; pamphlets; pictures,; clippings; periodicals; films and film strips; slides; wire; tape; phone; cassettes - audio-visual; floppies; CDs, DVDs; etc.

(f) **Location of Documents :** Use of catalogues - Kinds of entries; arrangement of entries; location in the catalogue; Call Number - Parts and role of each part; Arrangement of books on the shelves-Bay guides, shelf guides, inclusive numbers on the tier, arrangement and spine labels; identification of the book; etc.

(g) **Reference Books :** Characteristics, Kinds - Encyclopedias; Dictionaries, atlases, almanac, guide books, gazetteers, biographical dictionaries, indexes, etc.

(h) **Bibliography :** Selection of items, arrangement, preparation of index cards etc.

(iii) Other Activities : Other extension activities or user education programmes that a library may take-up to bring books and users together are :

(a) **Organisation of Exhibitions :** This will help in bringing to the notice of the users the richness of the collection of the library. Topical exhibitions will attract large number of users and will provide an opportunity to discover books which were not expected of.

(b) **Display of New Additions :** Many libraries display the jackets of the new additions at the entrance of the library so that they can draw the attention of the users and thus tempted to read. Some libraries may start a 'Monthly Book Exhibition' wherein, books added in the previous months are displayed from 1-10 of every month. This may provide an opportunity for users to have a look at books on all subjects at one place. Inter-disciplinary nature of the research support such displays.

(c) **Lectures :** Libraries should arrange topical lectures suitable to different sections of the users - men, women, children, students, etc. This opportunity should also be utilized for arranging suitable exhibitions/display of books and other reading material which help the users to select the right book for extended reading. Dr Ranganathan used to bring out topical bibliographies also on such occasions and distribute them among the listeners so that they can easily select literature on their choices of subject.

(d) **Other Extension Activities :** Many public libraries are also organizing dramas, musical concerts, film shows, quiz programmes, elocution and essay competitions, etc. to attract the public to the library and finally become beneficiaries of its resources.

(e) **Mass Media and Communication Technology :** In this context, mass media can be exploited in spreading the message - by writing articles in newspapers and magazines; radio and television talks; organizing public lectures; demonstration tours; attractive sign boards; organizing exhibitions; observing library weeks; publishing brochures; leaflets; bulletins; etc. The CDs etc. of user education programmes can be created and be shown at periodic occassion to the users to educate them.

(f) **Adult Education Programmes :** As a part of the extension programmes, library enthusiasts were organizing adult education classes to make the public literate so that they could make use of the libraries. Even today many of the public libraries are conducting adult education programme.

(h) **Local Broadcasting :** Village libraries may organise film shows, audio and videobroadcasts, lecture programmes, etc., in order to enlighten the illiterate public in terms of health, hygiene, family welfare, agriculture, culture and heritage, contemporary politics and economics, etc.

(i) **Reading Newspapers and Display of Wall-Newspapers :** Libraries in the villages, in localities where there is a considerable number of literate population may read newspapers and magazine articles of interest for illiterate public at specific hours in the morning and evening, during those hours where majority of them have a free time.

For the benefit of neo-literates, libraries do prepare wall-newspapers and display in the library as well as at places where majority of the public congregates.

Information Technology and User Education

It is seen during the last two decades that computers are increasingly being used for information activities, which has resulted in rapid growth of computer-based on-line information retrieval systems. Databases and computer stored information files are produced by many organizations such as American Chemical Society (Chemical Abstracts) and the US National Library of Medicine (Index Medicus) etc. These databases are now widely accessible for information searching from local terminals which are interlinked via Internet. Such efforts have resulted in the development of a number of on-line information retrieval systems. The use of these systems depends on the education of users and the availability and functioning of this method of information retrieval.

Different groups are concerned in on-line orientation, training and education. They are :

(i) Database producers

(ii) System operators

(iii) Institutions responsible for terminal operation, for example, libraries or information centres

(iv) Library schools

(v) Intermediaries and

(vi) End users

The motivation for each of these groups is expected to vary considerably to enable the end-user to carry out on-line information searches either himself or with the help of an intermediary, within his own subject field, as and when required, in connection with information needs and to enable an intermediary to carry out on-line information searches, for end-users, within many different subject fields, from the available databases, on the various information retrieval systems.

As far us user education with regards to on-line retrieval is concerned, it is an interactive process, particular attention needs to be paid to methods which permit the display and experience of this interaction.

In order to demonstrate on-line information retrieval, it is necessary to be able to show moving images generated in the computer search, thereby creating a feeling of reality. The ultimate aim of on-line instruction, for both end-users and intermediaries, is to be able to carry out on-line information searches. There, it is necessary to show moving images generated in the computer search, thereby creating a feeling of reality. The ultimate aim of on-line instruction, for both end-users and intermediaries, is to be able to carry out on-line information searches. Therefore, it is essential to practise on a real systems. This forms part of 'learning by doing' concept, which is also important in other forms of library user eduction. The need for live on-line instruction has been recognised by systems operators, who have provided various aids for teaching. In MEDLINE system, for example, the user can interactively ask for instructions at the beginning of the search, or for assistance during the search, when part of the instructions at the beginning of the search, or for assistance during the search, when part of the instructions are given as requested. The SDC (System Development Corporation) provides an on-line database over databases, DBI (Data Base Index) where the user can type in the subject area of interest and receive information as to the appropriate databases ranked in order of suitability for searching.

One of the most common ways of providing training for intermediaries is by letting them observe and work with a trained searcher. This is considered to be an essential part of intermediary training.

Besides, training is also essential when user is surfing the Internet and wants to get information through search engines.

Real 'hands-on' training in on-line searching is an important element in the education of end-users in computerized information retrieval. This would enable the students/users to be motivated and involve themselves actively in the learning process.

User Studies

The user studies are analogous to the efforts of a manufacturer who surveys his market for the product that he proposes to produce. In the context of a library and information system, it is extremely important that in-depth studies are conducted to acquire the actual and potential needs of users. On the basis of user studies, the collection building, processing and organization and service are assessed to justify itself for its existence.

The following methods are used for user studies.

1. Direct Method

The efforts in user studies so far have been confined to studying the user needs in the context of research and development in universities and industrial research units. The direct methods have emerged in recent decades to supplement the data acquired by indirect methods, that is, to analyse library records, to obtain data in the use of materials and user categories. Direct methods can be broadly studied under the following broad groups.

(i) Information gathering habits

(ii) Reading habits

(iii) Service preferences

(iv) Flow of information among users

(i) Information Gathering Habits : Information gathering habits are studied in the context of research and development. It is generally noted that researchers gather information in a number of ways such as :

— browsing current journals and also noting down the latest references to research papers.

— consulting, indexing and abstracting periodicals.

— contacting and obtaining information from persons in the same field.

— seeking information from tutors, guides and senior co-workers.

— writing to information supply centres and so on.

The efforts in trying to find out how a user obtains his information is to study the researcher's dependence on libraries, technical staff in the library and the main journals through which the researcher obtains the information. These studies have enabled library and information professionals to know the general behaviour of the researchers in obtaining their information, which in turn help them to organize their acquisition programmes, oriented towards actual requirements and to generate appropriate services.

(ii) Reading Habits : Reading habits of users of libraries throw considerable light on the types of documents a user studies, his relative preferences to the different categories of documents, frequency of borrowing and such other data. It is also possible for the library staff to study the time taken by a user for searching literature, browsing and reading. The data obtained in such studies help the organization to operate the library, in terms of user needs, physical location of documents, display of current journals, identification of intensive users of libraries, the types of documents frequently consulted and many others.

(iii) Service Preference : The library offers a variety of services which have evolved in the course of several decades. The normal lending, reference, bibliographic, hard copy supplies, etc. have been offered conventionally for a long time. More recently libraries and documentation centres have been offering Current awareness Services, Selective Dissemination of Information Services (SDI), Consolidation and Repackaging Services and so on.

It would be a waste of time, if these special services are organized indiscriminately without knowing the user preferences. It has now become, therefore, a practice to ascertain what kinds of service would be preferred by the users. Presently only those services which are of any consequence to the users are offered.

(iv) Information Flow : Research information generated by an individual or a group, gradually gets disseminated through personal correspondence, meetings at national and international conferences, publications in current journals or in the form of pre-prints and so on. It would be useful to know what medium is preferred by the generators of information for their propagation, to what extent conventional media like printed periodicals helping the dissemination and whether languages pose any barrier in communication, etc. These aspects are studied in information flow from generation to its final destination. These studies have thrown considerable light on the distribution of responsibilities among the different groups of disseminators, such as, the generator of information, the researcher and the editor, the publisher and the printer, the documentalists and information specialist and librarians. This has enabled these groups to organize their efforts with a sense of understanding of their responsibilities and ensuring smooth flow of information.

In the study conducted by the Operations Research Group of the Case Institute of Technology, USA in 1958 and by the Advisory Council of Science Policy in association with the department of Scientific and Industrial Research (UK), some interesting facts were found, which are given here.

(I) User requirements are of four types:

(a) current approach

(b) everyday approach

(c) exhaustive approach

(d) catching-up or brushing-up approach.

Current approach implies search for current literature. Every day approach means browsing through literature arrived at the library every day. Exhaustive approach entails search for exhaustive coverage of literature. Catching-up approach is the one that updates the knowledge of the user in any particular discipline consulting current journals and review journals.

(II) Library resources, library staff and the library services are generally revealed to be under-exploited by the users.

(III) Researchers spend about half of their working time in activities such as, browsing, reading, collection of references, talking or listening to co-workers, or fellow scientists.

(IV) The average number of journals scanned regularly by the researcher is less than 10.

(V) Scientists gather information mostly from their colleagues, teachers, group leaders, etc., and very less from libraries or secondary sources of information.

(VI) Scientists prefer review periodicals more than abstracting and indexing periodicals.

2. Indirect Methods

While direct methods of assessing user needs involve interface of investigators with users, the indirect methods analyse various types of records of a library, maintained on the use and users of the library. Another useful data which pertains to the bibliographical references that a researcher appends to his paper, provides considerable scope for analysis to get indicators for the management of the library. Indirect methods further can be sub-divided as under :

(i) Analysis of Library records : Libraries generally maintain statistical records on the different services it provides, such as, lending including inter-library loan, reference services, compilation of bibliographies, supply of facts, etc. Analysis of these records reveals the nature of use and documents, users needs, types of question posed, gaps and redundancies in book and journal collection, efficiency of reference and documentation services and similar others. This method has been used for a very long time to determine the policies of library in relation to collection building, organization of reader services, introduction of modern gadgets for speedy and efficient service etc.

(ii) Citation Analysis : Bibliographic citations appended to articles contributed by an author in a journal article, provides very useful data on the types of documents cited. This type of analysis helps in determining the acquisition policy, particularly of journals, and in weeding out less important ones. The citation studies also provide very useful indicators for indentifying institutions of excellence, individual experts and similar others.

3. Survey Methods

To explore information needs of users, their information gathering habits, reading habits, etc., various survey methods are prevalent. Some of the more important methods are :

(i) Questionnaire

(ii) Interview

(iii) Diary

(iv) Observation

(i) Questionnaire : In questionnaire method, the objectives of the survey are converted into simple and unambiguous questions. The questions posed relate to the user with reference to his name, designation and qualifications, experience and place of work etc. The other questions relate to the sources of information that the researcher consults and the way in which he obtains information from documentary and non-documentary sources. Preference is given to any type of information service and similar others. The questions are framed in such a way that the answers to most of them can be more or less 'yes or no' type without any necessity for detailed descriptions.

In this method, the cost of conducting a survey is very low and a large sample scattered over long distances can be covered. But sometimes, the response is usually poor and very often replies are incomplete, illegible and also manipulated. Besides, quite often the respondents fail to understand the merit of the questions properly and hence give incorrect replies.

(ii) Interview : Here, the investigator personally contacts the respondent and elicits the required information from him. The interview is taken either through a structured or unstructured questionnaire. In the structured questionnaire, all the questions are set prior to the interview, and the respondent is asked by the investigator to give replies to the questions. Either the investigator notes down the replies or the respondent himself writes down the replies. Whenever the respondent does not understand a question, the investigator explains the same, and the correct answer to the question is obtained. In the unstructured questionnaire, the investigator does not possess a set of questions already framed. On the other hand, he goes to the respondent keeping in view his objectives, and accordingly asks questions and notes down the answers. This methods is found to be more flexible than the structured one. This method however, is costly, labourious and time-consuming, since one has to contact personally or through representatives, all the respondents spread all over the country. Of course, it won't prove costly if the respondents are the users of a single library.

(iii) Diary : In this method, a diary of all the information activities by the user for a specified period of time. Initially a diary form is framed indicating all possible information activities of a user, i.e., literature search, browsing, reading, library use, discussion with experts etc., and supplied to the users. The users maintain the diary for the specified period and then hand this diary over to the investigator for analysis. The method proves to be successful if the diary keeping period is short, say one week or ten days.

(iv) Observation : Two types of observations methods i.e., participants and non- participants are known. When the observer participates with the group under study, it is called participant observation, and when the observer observes the activities of the group/ individual from a close distance, it is call non-participant observation. A particular observer makes himself a part of the group and takes part freely in the activities of the group and observes them in their natural behaviour, without allowing the individuals in the group to know that they are being observed. The information required is noted down and finally analysed.

A non-participant observer on the other hand, observes a selected number of user from a close distance and keeps a record of their information activities like time spent by user in library, types of documents he consults, number of documents he takes on loan and so on. Data gathered in this way are finally analysed.

4. Other Methods

These comprise of following sub-methods.

(i) Feed-back Service : A library can acquire feedback information on the variety of services it provides. In the organization of Selective Dissemination of Information Service, every document supplied to the customer is appended with a feedback data card which contains questions as to the relevancy of information, timeliness of supply and the descriptors use, etc. The analysis of such feedback data cards throws light on the efficiency of service and also provide considerable clue to build up pertinent user profiles.

(ii) Information Days : Information days are organized in many libraries which provide the occasion for the users to come in close contact with the library staff. This creates a better understanding between the users and the suppliers of information in the library and creates a sense of cordiality and brings a certain amount of credibility to the library. This practice is seen in the Soviet Union (now Russia), where on a particular day of a month, the library has an 'open day' and obtains direct feedback from the users on its services and collection. This method had enabled the libraries in the Soviet Union to improve their quality of service.

(iii) Unconventional Methods : Autobiographics or accounts of library users, such as scholars and writers provide useful hints as to their own experience in the collection of information. This study throws interesting light on the users' approach to information and provide pointers which may not be possible to obtain through any investigation. It should be noted, however, that this method is rather unusual and may or may not fetch any additional data at all.

In this way, opting any one or the other methods, user studies are done in the libraries.

9
Library Profession and Library Associations

Q. : Discuss Librarianship as a profession.

or

State the ethics of librarianship as a profession.

Ans. : Libraries have been considered as social institutions because they promote social interaction, entertainment and knowledge and have become an inseparable part of the society. Any change in the society is thus reflected as a reflection on the institution closely associated with it i.e., the libraries. These are the libraries that have built a strong or a weak nation, institution or an individual. In this modern world where the ambulance is overflooded with escalating prices, population, explosion knowledge, explosion technology, advancements and the urge and the need to explore the unknown and capture the known exerts tremendous pressure on the expansion of the structural as well as objective goal and outlook of the libraries.

In earlier days, the libraries were considered merely the store-houses and not much emphasis was on the usage of the material, on the contrary, its safe preservation was of prime importance. But slowly with the advent of printing and paper, more and more of printed material was stored and the library became a place where one could walk in to find any material that has been stored in published or unpublished form that is acquired by the library.

The development of libraries from mere storehouses, depositories to documentation and information centres is a very progressive one. The main factor for the development of library systems has been the tremendous increase in information caused by literature explosion, resulting into a choice situation. New processes and services were evolved to combat the existing problem. This new environment, full of various forms of literature saw the dawn of service oriented processes viz. bibliographical services, SDI services reprographic services and translation services. A new phase of library activities started taking place which was service oriented. There was a shift from books that were meant for preservation and storage to books that are to be used. With this the libraries were also concerned with collecting the documents but also had to work on modes and means of providing the documents to the concerned users well in time. The time constraint became very crucial as the researches were conducted at a very fast pace and with researches taking place at an international level the availability of documents at the right time was very important. In order to make this possible the libraries had to depend more on documentation activities and the emphasis on documents also saw a major change as the researches and scholars seemed to require the information exactly instead of going through the documents. Thus, the responsibility of the libraries further became intense, as the information within the various documents were to be sorted out according to the need of the users. All this changed the form and structure of the earlier known storehouses to documentation centers and information centers. Now, these centers took charge of supplying the required information to the required users through its services and saw that the sources of information were retrieved using the latest technologies so that delay of any kind could be avoided.

Information Technology has been a major factor in the development of the library system. The advent of computers and its application in libraries have totally given the libraries a fresh look. It has affected all the major areas viz.

— Collection

— Processing

— Services

As a result of the technology advancements, there has been a change in the storage devices due to a shift from print media to electronic media. This enables the information to be stored in electronic form in the various forms viz., floppies, CD-ROMs. Storage becomes easy as well as handling them is convenient too, and the services that are provided utilizing these storage devices are also very handy. The activities of the libraries like acquisition, circulation, cataloguing, serial control etc. can all be easily managed by the different software packages being developed for facilitating the library activities as well as providing prompt and error free services. All these activities have been supplemented by bar-coding technology, which is proving to be a technique that can be used for an efficient work.

Besides, Internet has by made its presence felt in all important sectors of human activities. The services and the amount of assistance that it has extended are adding a new dimension to the academic world.

Librarianship as a Profession

Library profession is a service oriented profession with distinguished liabilities and responsibilities. The code of professional ethics also describe that "The goal of librarianship is to mediate between humanity and humanity's store of recorded knowledge and information; to encourage and informed, enlightened and empowered citizenry; and to join with others in the fight for intellectual freedom and access to information." To build up this image for the library and information profession and to establish quality, a set of ethical codes has to be formulated and is to be practiced by librarians and information professionals.

Generally recognized professions, such as medicine, law, etc. have certain characteristics or attributes that are enumerated below :

- Extensive period of training;
- Dominance of intellectual component in work activities;
- Expertise;
- Service orientation;
- Altruistic motivation;
- Self motivation; and
- Autonomy.

Taking into consideration these sets of criteria, librarianship cannot, perhaps, be placed on par with the more well-established professions like medicine, law accountancy, etc. However, there is certainly a clear-cut body of professional techniques in librarianship that would involve its recognition as a profession. Librarianship in various degree fulfills some of the other characteristics like intellectual component, expertise, service of orientation, altruistic motivation, self motivation and autonomy.

The profession of librarianship in recent decades, has witnessed enormous changes, widening its scope and coverage, due to the application of information technology, rapidly expanding information needs of users and unprecedented increase in the volume and variety of available information coupled by social changes. The society today is moving through a transition period where the society is heading towards, information society, or global village. All these developments and the era of convergence tend to exert pressure on the society as it molds itself to absorb them for a prosperous future. These advancements in turn put pressure on the information centers as demands of the users are more specified and prompt replies are expected. To achieve this the library professionals need to opt themselves with the changing scenes so that the requirements of the clienteles are fulfilled in accordance to their demands.

Changing Dimension of the Profession

The role of earlier librarians was merely as a custodian or storekeeper who was concerned with the preservation and conservation of books. Slowly with more people evolving themselves in education and research activities, the role of librarian demands the provision of reference kind of information. Services like ready reference service and long-range reference services were developed to resolve the situational needs. It had the feature of providing books personally to the scholars for assisting them in their activities. The readers were provided bibliographic services to guide them in their research work.

As the emphasis on research grew supplemented by the governments assistance and the increase in the persons conducting research activities, exerted pressure on the existing services and demanded for personalized services and current information services assisted by abstracts, indexes, translations as well as reprographic facilities. The documentation service was to be provided to scholars engaged in progressive research activities for the development of a nation, thus the services needed specialities to be subject experts as well as service oriented, this lead to the creation of a more qualified set of persons to handle this situation known as Documentation officers or Information Officer. These officers as they handled information more and provided information to the anticipated users as well as on demand were preferred to be called Information Officers.

Now-a-days, a new and wider term Information Manager in popular usage is coming mainly due to the fact that, what the information officers dealt with was actually the management of information. The work began with the location of information in the different sources and forms and trying to make it accessible to the users utilizing the latest technologies so that they may have quicker access to it. Along with this, various services were also emphasized to enable the proficient use of the resources.

The advancement in technologies also provided us with different management softwares that made the functioning of libraries more systematic. The entire process of the library activities was converted into a management program. In order to use them, very user friendly software were developed that made library management more systematic and efficient.

The changing trends brought forward information available in variant forms and in diverse sources viz. floppies, CD-ROM, Multimedia, hypertext, on-line, etc. All these developments made the availability of information both nascent and retrospective, without loss of time, thus, the management of information became a difficult task and important requirement, too. So, todays, the library professionals are expected to act as Information Manager rather than the Traditional Libraries.

Professional Ethics in librarianship

Professional ethics is considered as an expression of ethos (i.e. character, culture, spirit, practice) of an occupation. It means that the values attached to a profession that makes it meaningful. It is the responsibility of each and every professional to abide by the values related to their occupation so that they can do justice to their profession.

It is easy to think of ethical values as essential to ensure quality of professional performance, it is very difficult to design a universally acceptable standard code for professional ethics. Individual/personal ethics are fundamental to any set of ethical codes which are not explicitly stated in any professional end, as they are very often assumed to the basic to every situation. There are also differences in the conception of ethical behaviour in different societies and cultures. In order to be effective, therefore, professional ethics have to be perceived at various levels, appropriate to different cultures and situations. These levels may be at the primary, institutional, professional, national and international levels. Primary levels are a set of basic guiding principles which are fundamental to human behaviour with reference to any activity, such as honesty, good conduct, adherence to truth and so on.

In general ethics means a set of moral principal/rules. These rules may be rules of conduct recognized by a particular group or with respect to a particular class of human activities. Ethics as defined by Websters International Dictionary is as :

— the discipline dealing with what is good and bad or right and wrong with moral duty and obligation.
— a group of moral principles or set of values; a particular theory or system or moral values; the principles of conduct governing an individual or a profession; standards of behaviour.

As far as the librarianship is concerned, John Bekker, suggested some broad outlines or the framing of a code of professional ethics as under :

— Librarians should exercise their best professional judgment on behalf of users.
— Librarians should strive to improve libraries and library services.
— Librarians should help create and maintain conditions under which learning and scholarship can flourish, freedom of inquiry and of though and its expression.
— Librarians should be sensitive to the concerns of the larger society, of which they are a part.

Attempts at designing a code of professional ethics for librarianship have been made by some of the professional bodies as :

ALA Ethical Code

The American Library Association, adopted a professional code in 1938. The ALA Ethical code defined the relation of librarians to :

— the governing authority;
— their constituency;
— their fellow employees within the library;
— their profession; and
— Society.

The national debate, however, on the articles relating to the above stated areas went on in the next decades. In 1975, ALA adopted a new Statement on Professional Ethics which replaced the 1938 code. Later in the same year, the ALA Council instituted and authorized a standing committee on professional ethics to augment the Statement on Professional Ethics by explanatory interpretations and additional statements. At the ALA membership meeting in 1981, the Code of Ethics was officially adopted. Responding to numerous criticisms on the 1981 Code, the ALA Standing Committee on Professional Ethics decided to proceed towards further revision.

A draft code of Ethics for Library and Information Professionals was published by the American Association for Information Science in 1990. This code constituted a preamble and four categories of ethical responsibilities to :

— Individuals
— Society
— the sponsor
— the employer; and
— the profession

LA's Code of Professional Conduct

In 1978, the Working Party on Professional Ethics was established within the United Kingdom's Library Association to develop a draft code of ethics. A draft was prepared for discussion and debate in 1980; the final version of the code, the Code of Professional Conduct was adopted by the Council of the UK Library Association at its 100th Annual General Meeting in 1983. The Code includes the procedures and regulatory actions that will follow a breach of the code by a member of the Library Association.

The features of the Code relate to:

(a) the competency of the librarian;
(b) the question of discretion and respect of a client's privacy;
(c) professional independence and intellectual freedom;
(d) the impartiality of the library profession;
(e) financial ethics; and
(f) the integrity of members.

In addition to the above regulations, the LA's code of professional conduct has introduced an implementation mechanism that involves sanctions imposed by the LA's Disciplinary Committee on those who do not abide by the rules of conduct set by the code.

Indian Situation

In India, the subject of professional ethics in librarianship is still to be recognized as a necessity. The only effort to consider this subject seriously in a professional forum appears, to be at the IASLIC Conference in 1984. There were ten papers presented at the Conference, five of these give a good overview of professional ethics, four on professional ethics for persons working in university, special and other institutional libraries, and another on Ranganathan's Five Laws vis-a-vis professional ethics with special reference to a research library. All these papers have a good number of references which would facilitate further readings on the subject.

Concluding, it can be said that the new evolving trends demands an expressive change in modern librarianship and with the intrusion of IT we find a tremendous change engulfing our profession. In the present context it becomes essential for the library professionals to identify the skill and competencies required to suit the new environment. Some of the skill would include having sound knowledge of the subject, ability to negotiate, persuade, build teams, influence, provide leadership supplemented by skills of resource management, organization of knowledge, analysis and understanding of related areas. To combat with the evolving scenario, the library professionals need to redefine their present status and acquire new skill that are requites of the modern society.

Q. : Write down the aims and objectives of professional associations in the field of library and information service.

or

Explain the role of Indian Library Association (ILA) in promoting professional activities in the field of library in India.

or

Explain the role of any International Association in the field of Library Science.

Ans. : A lone professional or a single institution cannot possibly do much to deal with wider and far reaching issues of professional concern rather a collective action by interested groups is necessary. In this, professional associations serve as a forum for coordinated efforts. Library development is dependent upon professional planning, far sight, understanding and involvement. These are taken much better care of by library associations than individual institutions. During the last hundred years bonds between librarians and library practitioners developed and took the shape of formal associations with the remarkable growth of librarianship is a profession. Librarians organised themselves into general and specific associations, which provided a corporate personality and a voice for its individual members.

Aims and Objectives of Library Associations

The aims and objectives of a library association may be :

— hearld library movement in a country to spread knowledge and information and ultimately contribute to human resources development;

— work for enactment of public library legislation, drafting of the bills along progressive lines based on sound principles; make the people library conscious so that they demand their rights to access to public library services; mobilise social pressure for healthy development of library services;

— strive for an evolution of a versatile, integrated national library and information system based on a national policy; bring the attention of authorities to deficiencies, defects, distortions, etc. in the existing library infrastructure;

— provide a common forum for library professionals for exchange of information, ideas, experiences and expertise; work for betterment of salary, grades, service conditions, status, etc. of library professionals;

— hold the image of the library profession high in the society; promote cooperation among libraries and library professionals;

— towards sharing of resources and avoiding duplication of efforts;

— contribute towards manpower development for library and information work that includes education and training, research, incentives, awards and rewards, etc.

Functions of Library Associations

Depending upon the stages of development, library associations usually perform following functions :

— Undertake surveys of library facilities and services, user demands, reading habits, book production, etc. in order to identify strengths and weaknesses so us to take necessary steps to improve the system,

— Organize user education programmes, library week, exhibitions, book fairs, competitions, etc. for promoting library consciousness and reading habits among the people,

— Take up with managements at all levels through appropriate means, issues relating to betterment of salary grades, service conditions and status of library professionals.

— Frame code of ethics for library professionals in order to preserve high values in conduct and service.

— Conduct training courses that are necessary to supplement university education in library and information science and continuing education programmes for working professionals.

— Function as an accrediting body to maintain proper standards in library and information science education,

— Institute awards and rewards to recognize outstanding performance of library professionals and library systems,

— Setup a placement cell to help in recruitment of library personnel, Organizing conferences, seminars, lectures colloquial, etc. to afford opportunities for the professionals to meet, discuss and exchange information, ideas, experiences and expertise,

— Publish a regular official periodical and a newsletter as well as adhoc publications such as proceedings, directories, catalogues, bibliographies, course manuals, textbooks, reference books, and others,

— Formulate standards, guidelines, codes and manuals with regard to practices, procedures, techniques, tools and equipment, as a step towards fostering cooperation among libraries,

— Undertake research and bibliographical projects on their own and through outside contract. Also may offer advisory and constancy services,

— Maintain liaison with book and publishing trade for attending to mutual problems in library acquisitions, and

— Establish cooperation with international and national associations of other countries having similar objectives.

LIBRARY ASSOCIATIONS IN INDIA

India has many national and state level library associations. Each state in India has an association. Some state library associations like Baroda Library Association (1910), Andhra Desa Library Association (1914), Bengal Library Associations (1927) and Madras Library Association (1927) has good beginings to encourage the formation of the Indian Library Association for co-ordinating their activities. Only a few associations are active in contributing to professional development. Professionals are generally indifferent to become members of library associations. The fact that many states have not enacted library legislation. There is however scope and need for better functioning and performance of our library associations. Madras and Mysore, Maharashtra and Andhra Pradesh Library Associations have succeeded in promoting legislation for establishing a network of libraries in respective states.

Prior to 1960, the activities of U.P. State Library Association was concerned mainly at Lucknow but since 1960, it has become an active organization. Two associations at the national level namely Indian Library Association (ILA) and Indian Association of Special Libraries and Information Centers (IASLIC) are working well; these are described as under :

1. Indian Library Association (ILA)

The birth of ILA association can be traced to the holding of an ALL India Library Conference at Calcutta in September 1933. All leading librarians of Baroda, Rampur, Punjab, Bengal State Library Associations and Madras, Bombay, Banaras Universities were instrumental in organizing the conference. The first all Indian Library conference was held in the Asiatic Society Hall, Calcutta on 12th September 1933. It was at this conference that Indian Library Association was formally established on 13th September 1933. It is a registered society, with headquarters now located at Delhi. It is the premier national association representing the entire library profession in the country.

(a) Objectives : The objectives of the association are :

(i) Promotion of library movement and improvement in library services in all aspects in the country.

(ii) Promotion of library science education and improvement in the training of librarians in the country.

(iii) Promotion of bibliographical study and research in library science.

(iv) Improvement in the state and conditions of service of librarians.

(v) Affiliation with the state and other library associations and cooperation with international and other national associations with similar objectives.

(vi) Publication of bulletins, periodicals and other publications which will lend to the realization of the objectives of the association.

(vii) Providing a common forum by organizing conferences, seminars and meeting etc.

(viii) Promotion and formulation of standards, norms, guidelines, etc. for management library and information systems and services.

(b) Organisation : The membership of the Association comprises patrons, honorary members, life and ordinary members, and Institutional and Associate members. The General Body elects, for a two-year term, a President, Six Vice-Presidents, a General Secretary and Council Members up to 20 at the rate of one representative for every 100 personal members and as many at the rate of one representative for every 40 institutional members. There are 11 Sectional Committees to look after professional work in different areas. The Chairman of the Sectional Committees, one representative of each member state library association and Presidents of the Association are also members of the Council. An Executive Committee consisting of the President, one Vice-President, the General Secretary, the Treasurer, two Secretaries, P.R.O. and three Council Members, look after routine management. While the General Body meets once in a year, usually at the time of All India Library Conference, the Council meets at least once in a quarter and the Executive Committee as often as necessary. The Annual Report and Accounts of the Association are passed at the General Body Meeting.

(c) Activities : ILA's activities are confined mainly to the following areas :

— **Meetings :** An All India Conference is held every year in different parts of the country at the venue of host institutions which are usually universities, institutions and local library association.

— **Continuing Education Programme :** The association has taken initiative in continuing educating programme for the benefit of library professionals to upgrade their knowledge and skills. Recognizing the curricular changes in library schools, the associations has endeavored to fill the gap by conductive short term training courses in the latest areas. Since 1986, the association in collaboration with NISSAT/DSIR and similar other bodies has started workshop for the benefit of the members.

— **Relations with Other Professional Bodies :** ILA plays a leading role in the Joint Council of Library Associations in India towards evolving a coordinated approach and a common strategy on professional issues of concern to all library associations. It has good working relations with IASLIC and state library associations. The association is represented in Raja Ram Mohan Roy Library Foundation, Good offices committee, the National Bureau of Standards, National Book Trust etc. Association is also a member of IFLA and the common wealth Library Association.

— **Library Legislation :** The association has been working to improve and expand public library services since 1933 by organizing the annual conference, special symposia, seminars, library week etc. The association has been pressing the government at the centre and in the states to bring forth paper on library legislation, without which it is not possible to have well planned public library system in the country.

— **Publications :** ILA brings following publications :

— ILA Bulletin

— ILA Newsletter

— ILA membership Directory

— Directory of Libraries in India

The Association also brings out regularly its Annual Report and Statement of Accounts.

ILA is now firmly organized, with confidence of the library profession assured, to carry on and expand its programmes and activities with a view to meet the hopes and aspirations of the profession and to serve the cause of librarianship and library service in the country.

2. Indian Association of Special Libraries and Information Centres (IASLIC)

With the dawn of India's independence, impetus was given to

research in science and technology by increased financial grants to postgraduate departments of universities and by establishment of national laboratories of Council for Scientific and industrial Research (CSIR), Defense Research Laboratories, and Indian Institute of Technology at Kharagpur, Bombay, Madras Kanpur and Delhi. This led to the realization of lacuna in the collection and dissemination of scientific and knowledge information. To overcome this, an attempt was made to set up a special library association in 1949. It took another 6 years for the actual establishment of such a professional body.

The Indian Association Special Libraries and Information Centres (IASLIC) was founded in 1955. It is a registered society, with headquarters located at Kolkata. It was formed with the aim of having an association in India similar to the Association for Information Management in UK and the Special Libraries Association in USA.

Dr. S.L. Hora was the first President of IASLIC, and Mr. J. Saha, the chief librarian of the Indian Statistical Institute, Calcutta was Honorary Secretary.

(a) Objectives : The objectives of the association are :

(i) to encourage and promote the systematic acquisition, organization and dissemination of knowledge ;

(ii) to improve quality of library and information services and documentation work ;

(iii) to coordinate the activities of and to foster mutual cooperation and assistance among the special libraries, scientific, technological and research institutions, learned societies, commercial organizations, industrial research establishments as well as other information and documentation centres to the fullest extent;

(iv) to serve as field of active contact for libraries, information bureaus, documentation centres, scientists, research workers, specialists and others having common interest ;

(v) to improve the technical efficiency of the workers in special library and information and documentation centres and to look after their professional welfare;

(vi) to act as a centre of research in special library and documentation techniques ;

(vii) to act as a centre of information in scientific, technical and other fields ;

(viii) to take all such action as may be incidental or conducive to the attainment of the objects of the association or any of them.

(b) Organisation : The membership of IASLIC consists of honorary members, life and ordinary members and the institutional members. The General Body elects, for a two-year term, a President, six Vice-Presidents, a General Secretary, a Treasurer, two Joint Secretaries, two Assistant Secretaries, a Librarian and 20 Council Members. The Council appoints from among its members, the Executive and Finance Committees. The work of the Association is distributed among six divisions with specific responsibilities assigned to them.

(c) Activities : IASLIC's activities are confined mainly to the following six areas:

— **Meetings :** IASLIC holds a biennial seminar and a conference in alternate years in different parts of the country at the venue of host organisations who are usually university libraries/ departments of library and information science, institutions, associations etc. It has recently formed four special interest groups devoted to areas like Industrial Information, Social Science Information, Computer Application and Humanities They meet at the of annual conference/seminar to discuss problems of common interest. IASLIC also organizes from time to time adhoc seminars, lectures, exhibitions, etc. It has formed Study Circles at Kolkata and other cities. The meetings of the study circles are held every month, wherein technical issues are discussed.

— **Conference, Seminars and Training Programme:** IASLIC has always been a dynamic association regularly holding seminars and conferences on topics of current and vital importance. It has published the working papers with the proceedings of these seminars.

— **Continuing Education Programme:** The education division organized special courses on different topics for updating library professional and library science teachers to the latest information technologies. IASLIC has conducted over 35 courses on computer applications to library and information system covering various aspects such and CDS/ISIC retrieval system, information management, information consolidation, thesaurus in information retrieval and use of audio visual materials.

— **Bibliography and Translation Services:** IASLIC offers translation and bibliography compilation services to individuals and institutions on a non-profit basis. It maintains library devoted to library and information science literature.

— **Publications :** It brings out following publications :

- IASLIC Bulletin (Quarterly)
- IASLIC News letter (Monthly)
- Indian Library Science Abstract (ILSA) (Annual)

Besides, it brought out also the second edition of the Directory of Special and Research Libraries in India in 1985. It had brought out some monographs and one each of a manual, code and glossary. The Association also brings out regularly its Annual Report and Statement of Accounts and Membership List.

— **Relations with other Bodies:** IASLIC maintains a healthy relation with the Indian Library Association and other library associations. It has taken a leading part in the formation of the Joint Council for Library Associations in India. It takes an active interest in implementing the common programmes of this Joint Council for Library Association in India.

IASLIC has had satisfying accomplishments in playing a leader coordinator role in special library and information field in the country. It is now posed for an assured growth and development in the period ahead for serving the cause of special librarianship in India.

LIBRARY ASSOCIATION IN OTHER COUNTRIES

Two library associations, one of the United States of America and one of the United kingdom namely American Library Association and Library Association (UK), have a ling and distinguished record of activities and service. These and others are described below :

1. American Library Association (ALA)

The American Library Association was founded in 1876 by Melvil Dewey, Justin Winsor, A. Cutter, Samuel S. Green, James L. Whitney, Fred B. Perkins and Thomas W. Dicknell. At a meeting held in Philadelphia in the fall of 1876 to coincide with the nation' centennial celebration, resolved on a motion moved by Melvil Dewey, the father of librarianship, to form the American Library Association. It is the oldest and largest library association in the world with members in academic, public, school, government and special libraries. The association promotes the creation, maintenance and enhancement of learning society encouraging its members to work with educators, government officials and organizations in abolitions to intimate and support comprehensive efforts to ensure that school, public academic and special libraries in every community cooperate to provide lifelong learning services to all.

(a) Objectives : The main objective of the ALA is to provide leadership for the development promotion and improvement of library and information services and the profession of librarianship in order to enhance learning and ensure access to information for all.

(b) Organisation : Any person, library or other organization interested in library services and libraries is admitted as a member and there is no geographical limit. In 1999, ALA had on rolls 53,568 personnel and 3699 institutional members besides, 146 corporate members. ALA elects a President, a Secretary and other office-bearers. It is governed by a Council. The Executive Board is the management arm. It has at present a number of divisions such as those relating to adult services, libraries for children and young, library education, reference and adult services, and resources and technical services as well as committees devoted to various other subjects. In some areas, there are well developed associations working under the umbrella of ALA but functioning as separate divisions such as American Association of School Libraries, American Library Trustee Association, Association for Library Services to Children, Association of Specialised and Cooperative Library Agencies, Library Administration and Management Association, Library and Information Technology Association and Public Libraries Association. Yet another tier in the structure consists of Round Tables, which are membership units dealing with aspects of librarianship outside the scope of a division.

(c) Activities : The work of ALA is centred mainly on its divisions, committees and round tables. The Annual Conference of ALA is held usually in June in different cities. A number of pre and post-conference seminars, workshops, etc. are also held at that time.

— **Division :** ALA has 11 divisions; each division is responsible for a specified area of concern. Each division is with an elected board of directors and such committees and sections are required to accomplish the division's goals. The divisions are :

- American Association of School Librarians
- Association for Library Collections and Technical Services
- Association for Library Service to Children
- Association for Library Trustees and Advocates
- Association of College and Research Libraries
- Association of Specialized and Cooperative Library Agencies
- Library Administration and Management Association
- Library and Information Technology Association
- Public Library Association
- Reference and User Services Association
- Young adult Library Services Association

— **Committees :** Committees which are created by the executive board, council and the President are designated as committees of the association and committees of the council. These committees are responsible for areas affecting all library and association concerns.

— **Round Tables :** A round table is a membership unit established to promote a field of librarianship not within the scope of any single division. Each table is with an elected governing body, composed of members of the association. The association has 18 round tables.

- Armed Forces Libraries
- Continuing Library Education at Network Exchange
- Ethnic Materials Information Exchange
- EMIERT ALA
- Exhibits
- Federal Librarians
- Gay Lesbian, Bisexual and Transgendered Round Table
- Government Documents
- Intellectual Freedom

- International Relations
- Library History
- Library Instruction
- Library Research
- Map & Geography
- New Members
- Social Responsibilities
- Staff Organizations
- Support Staff Interests
- Video

- **Education and Training Programmes :** In education and training for librarianship, its role has been mainly accreditation and selling up of proper standards. However, its activities under continuing education programme are numerous. ALA has a creditable record in promoting and encouraging research, innovation, invention, etc. in the library and information science field. The library technology programme has contributed significantly. ALA has been quite active in the passage of federal legislation in matters relating to library services. Library Bill of Rights, Library Services Act of 1956 (amended in 1964) and legislations dealing with postal rates, copyright and funds for library services are examples of initiatives taken by ALA. It also takes interest in clarification of legislative issues whenever situation warrants.
- **Publications :**
  - ALA Handbook of Organisation
  - College and Research Libraries
  - College and Research Libraries News
  - Information Technology and Libraries Interface
  - Journal of Youth Services In Libraries
  - Knowledge Quest
  - Library Administration and Management
  - Library Resources and Technical Services
  - Public Libraries

– RUSA Update

Other units of ALA are also bringing out serial titles. Its ad hoc publications comprising monographs, manuals, guides, codes, handbooks, proceedings of annual conference etc. may extend to more than 2,000 titles and account for significant world library science literature. ALA has instituted several awards in the name of some eminent library scientist to encourage and recognise working professionals for outstanding performance and excellence in certain fields. The following are a few examples:

— John Cotton Dana Library Public Relations Award;

— Clearance Day Award for promoting love of books and reading;

— Melvil Dewey Award for creative professional achievement;

— E.P. Dutton-John McRae Award for advanced study for serving the needs of culturally deprived children;

— Margaret Mann Award for achievements in cataloguing and classification;

— Ralph R. Shaw Award

Besides, ALA has been active in international cooperation and relations. It also takes part in the programmes of UNESCO, IFLA and FID and has assisted many countries through advisory services, technical assistance, fellowships, travel grants, supply of reading materials, etc.

2. Library Association (LA-UK)

The Library Association (LA-UK) is another oldest and largest library association like the American Library Association, which was founded in 1877 with its headquarters in London. It was founded as the Library Association of the United Kingdom at the conclusion of the First International Conference of Librarians held at Brussels in October 1877. Later on 17 February 1898, Queen Victoria granted the Association a Royal Charter. In 1986, Queen Elizabeth-II granted a supplement charter which amended the purposes and powers in the original charter to reflect the association's contemporary role.

(a) Objectives : The objectives of the Library Association are primarily to unite all persons engaged or interested in library work and include promotion of the establishment and improvement of libraries, promotion of appropriate legislation, encouragement of research, better qualifications of librarians and raising of professional standards and conditions generally.

(b) Organisation : The membership of the Library Association is over 25,000 and is open to all interested in its aims and objectives. However, the status of Chartered Librarian and the use of the title of Associate of the Library Association (ALA) are restricted to those who have successfully completed the courses and training of the Association prescribed for the purpose. Fellowship of the Library Association is given on submission of an approved thesis for outstanding service to librarianship. The Library Association has twelve regional branches, including the Scottish and Welsh Library Associations and twenty three special interest groups. The Library Association is governed by a 60 number council elected by the members and is advised by four main committees: Executive Coordinating, General Purpose, Library Services and Professional Development and Education.

c. Activities : The major activities are :

— **Annual Conferences and Continuing Education Programmes:** The Association holds annual conference regularly. In addition, Branches and Groups arrange their own conferences, meetings and study schools. Printed proceedings usually result from these meetings. From its earliest years, the Library Association has been organizing courses for aspiring librarians, planning syllabus, conducting examinations, and maintaining a professional register. It has encouraged formation of library schools in the country. After the library schools were developed, LA's role as an examining body had diminished. But it still plays an important part in continuing professional education and training. It organizes an increasing number of short courses on currently important aspects of library and information science and carries on a continuing dialogue with library schools for maintaining high standards of library education.

— **Publications :** The Association publishes books, pamphlets, periodicals, book-lists, special subject lists, reprints, etc. with the aim of service to members and profession.

Periodicals and Serials :

- Library Association Record (Monthly)
- Liaison (Monthly)
- British Technology Index (Monthly)

- British Humanities Index (Monthly)
- British Education Index (Monthly)
- Library and Information Science Abstracts (Bi-Monthly)
- Journal of Librarianship (Quarterly)
- Library Association Yearbook
- Current Research in Library & Information Science (3 issues).

— **Relations with other Institutions :** The Library Association is represented in many official bodies and committees and has been offering advisory service and professional assistance in many programmes of library development. It had played a major role in the establishment of the British Library in 1973. Besides, the Library Association has helped information of the regional library system and promoted inter-library cooperation.

— **International Relations :** The Library Association collaborates with UNESCO, IFLA and FID and participates in their programmes towards international cooperation and exchange of experience and expertise. It assists the British Council in implementing its assistance programmes in developing countries. It organizes visits, study tours, fellowship programmes, etc., which are part of cultural exchange programmes. It is particularly active in relations with Commonwealth countries. It has helped to establish the Commonwealth Library Association.

— **Awards :**

- LA Carnegie Medal – for best children's book;
- LA Kate Greenaway Medal – for best illustrated children's book;
- LA Weathly Medal – for an outstanding index;
- LA Besterman Medal – for outstanding bibliography;
- LA Mc Colvin Medal – for an outstanding reference book.

Since 1986, the Association has been considering its future development and in this connection two reports, Futures-1 and Futures-2 have appeared. With a creditable record of performance in the past, and a well organised structure, the future of the Library Association is one of hope and promise.

3. Association for Information Management (ASLIB)

ASLIB owes its existence largely, but not exclusively to initiatives in the metallurgical industries where interest in technical literature and recognition of the need for its more systematic exploitation for industrial purposes were both strongly developed in the years following World War I. An exploratory conference held at Hoddesdon, Hertfordshire in 1926 with the modest purpose of providing an opportunity for an exchange of views on mutual assistance resulted in a decision to found a new association under the name Association of Special Libraries and Information Bureau (ASLIB). Thus, the ASLIB was founded in 1926 which earned a great reputation by its record of professional service. In 1983, however, the Association extended its activities, in tune with expanding dimensions of information and renamed it as the Association for Information Management. But as the Association was well known as ASLIB, it continues the same acronym to represent its new name also. The British Society for International Bibliography was merged into it in 1949.

ASLIB has been instrumental in focusing on the importance of information in all spheres of national endeavour, particularly in the reconstruction period after the World War II. By demonstrating its usefulness, ASLIB could secure the recognition of the British Government as a research association. The creation of the Office of Scientific and Technical Information, which was a forerunner to the British Library was largely due to the spade work done by ASLIB.

(a) Objectives : ASLIB aims to facilitate the coordination and systematic use of sources of knowledge and information in all public affairs and in industry and commerce and in all the arts and sciences. It aims to increase the contribution of information to the economic, social and cultural life of the community by the promotion of effective information management.

(b) Organisation : The membership of ASLIB is largely composed of corporate bodies, including industrial and business organizations, professional and learned societies, public, academic and national libraries, publishers and database providers. It has over 2,000 members, approximately a quarter of which are in countries other than the UK. Further, personal members may account for only one fourth of the membership only. It has branches in Scotland, the North of England and the Midlands. Subject groups have been formed in biological and agricultural sciences, chemistry, economic and business information, electronics, engineering, private view-data, transport and planning. There are also technique groups covering translations, informatics and computer application. A sub-group represents the interests of one-man-bands.

(c) Activities : The activities of the association include the followings :

— **Information Services :** The information services would also be reorganized to offer a higher level of practical advice and information to its members. The new information resources centres, besides offering a basic referral service, would advise the members on practical issues of information management in the following key areas :

  - online information retrieval methods and systems;
  - library automation.
  - networking, including local area networks;
  - software for library and information retrieval applications;
  - modern library/information resource management.

With the increase in the number of publicly accessible online databases, a need was felt to provide information about the databases. In 1979 ASLIB established its online information centre to provide enquiry service concerning the availability of databases on specific subjects, coverage of data, search strategy, and equipment and telecommunications. The centre publishes a monthly newsletter and all subscribers to the newsletter have access to enquiry service at no additional cost.

Besides, there are about 30,000 volumes in the ASLIB library. Most of these books are related to information science and documentation. ASLIB also provides photocopy service both to members and non-members. It keeps a register of specialist translators. Also maintain an index of articles on scientific and technical subjects translated into English.

— **Professional Development Programmes :** ASLIB organizes a number of short courses for both members and non-members. A wide range of topics are covered in the training programme. Most of them have practical value. In a year, as many as forty courses may be organized. On some topics, the courses are repeated many times. Attention is paid to courses in newly emerging areas. The training programme of ASLIB has earned recognition and is increasingly being taken advantage of.

— **Publication :** The serial publications of ASLIB are :

- ASLIB Proceedings (monthly)
- ASLIB Booklist (monthly)
- ASLIB Information (monthly)
- ASLIB Newsletter (monthly)
- Index to Thesis (annual)
- Journal of Documentation (quarterly)
- Netlink (3 issues)
- Program : News of Computers in Libraries (quarterly)
- Forthcoming International Scientific and Technical Conference (quarterly)
- Technical Translation Bulletin (3 issues)

ASLIB's occasional publications consist of monographs, directories, reports, proceedings, bibliographies, etc. The publications of ASLIB have a wide recognition and appeal for their content and standard. For example, ASLIB's Handbook of Special Librarianship and Information Work (Edn. 5, 1985) is widely distributed and serves as a valuable guide for developing library and information services and systems.

There has been a shift in emphasis in the objectives as well as in approaches to realize the objectives. Information management is now the core programme of ASLIB. Promotional role is less prominent. Nonetheless, ASLIB will continue to have its influence and impact in special library and library field in UK and elsewhere.

3. INTERNATIONAL ASSOCIATIONS

1. International Federation for Information and Documentation (FID)

International Federation for information and Documentation was founded by Paul Otlet and Henri La Fontaine in Belgium in 1895 as the International Institute of Bibliography (IIB). In 1930; it was renamed as International Federation for Documentation and as International Federation for Documentation and Information in 1986. At the time of its foundation, the main objective was the creation and maintenance of a comprehensive world repertory of knowledge and development of the Universal Decimal Classification from the Dewey Decimal Classification for providing order and access to bibliographical entries in the world repertory. While the Universal Bibliographic Repertory project had failed, the IIB left agencies of great value in providing a nucleus for evolution of FID and in the development of UDC which is still the world's major classification scheme for information and knowledge.

In the early period, its activities were few; it become a Federation in 1924 and got legal status in 1959 as international nongovernmental organization under the Belgian act granting incorporation to international non-profit associations pursuing a scientific, artistic or educational goal. In 1938, its headquarters were shifted to Hague. After world war II, there has been a gradual increase in membership and steady expansion of activities reflecting its international character.

For more than 100 years, FID has played a leading role in developing information and documentation techniques and services, and promoting the interest of information specialists and users, from around the world.

(a) Objectives : FID aims to:

(i) promote the study and application of information science, documentation and information management;

(ii) provide a forum for the dissemination and exchange of ideas, information, knowledge and skills among information and documentation professionals;

(iii) promote the professional development of information and documentation specialists;

(iv) promote and protect the interest of information users;

(v) promote international cooperation in the fields of information science, documentation and information management.

(b) Organization : The FID membership comprises of international and national members, institutional, corporate and personal members, and the honorary fellows. Among the institutions in FID membership, are national and international libraries and documentation centres, professional associations of information specialists, scientific arid technical information centres and services, academic institutions and their libraries and commercial firms. Individual members include academics, archivists, consultants, document lists, government officials, IT specialists, information scientists, journalists, lawyers, librarians policy makers, providers of information products and services, publishers, scientists, students and trainees. In 1999, special low rates were introduced for institutional and personal members in the least developed countries recognized as such by the United Nations.

As far as the structure is concerned, a General Assembly of national and international members which meets once in two years govern the activities of FID. Its membership comprises 69 national members, 3 international members and some 250 affiliates. Its secretariat functions from the Hague. It has an executive committee comprising a President, a permanent Secretary - General and a few senior officers. There is a council of elected national delegates of the General Assembly which elected national delegates of the General Assembly, responsible for implementation of policies of the Assembly.

FID Committees : Most of the work of FID is done in committees. These committees have a large number of 'sub-committees' and 'working groups'.

FID/RI	Research on the Theoretical Basis of information; Secretariat: Russia.
FID/CR	Classification Research; Secretariat: Denmark
FID/TM	Theory of Machine Techniques and Systems; Secretariat: Sweden.
FID/OM	Operational Machine Techniques and System; Secretariat: United Kingdom.
FID/LD	Linguistics in Documentation; Secretariat: United States
FID/II	Information for Industry; Secretariat: Denmark
FID/ET	Education and Training; Secretariat: Poland; from 1973-Federal Republic of Germany
FID/DC	Developing Countries; Secretariat: Hungary

The joint committees are :

FID/CIB	International Council for Building
FID/IAALD	International Association of Agricultural Librarians and Documentalists.

(c) Activities : The main activities include :

— **UDC Consortium :** Since its day as the Institute International de Bibliographic, the organization was largely responsible for the development and publication of the most sophisticated and multi-purpose general classification scheme, the Universal Decimal Classification (UDC). However, in 1992, the responsibility for the UDC was transferred to a non-profit consortium of publishers of different language version of the scheme one of which is FID.

— **Professional Network :** FID maintains and continually develops an international network of professionals throughout the world. These individuals and institutions represent a huge body of expertise to which all FID members have access. They include not only other FID members, but intergovernmental organizations, other international professional bodies, academic institutions and commercial firms, as well as individuals in many spheres of activity.

FID's website www.fid.in, provides a virtual portal to informal issues worldwide through hyperlinks with members and others, while LIS-FID's free listserver, enables members and other to keep up to date with today's key information issues.

— **Global Information Alliance (GIA) :** In 1995, FID played the leading role in establishing the GIA as an informal strategic alliance of over 35 leading international nongovernmental organizations and professional associations in the fields of information, communication and knowledge transfer. GIA members aim to better serve the world community by working together on a wide range of issues of common interest related to the management and use of information.

— **Conferences and Exhibitions :** FID organizes a biennial international conference and exhibitions as well as regional and national conferences, seminars, and workshops on a variety of professional themes. The 50th FID international conference and exhibition was held in Brasilia, Brazil 25-30, September 2000 on the theme - Knowledge without frontiers: a fundamental right for the new millennium.

— **Projects :** FID and its members conduct projects for international organization such as UNESCO, UNIDO, the commission of

European Communities, the International Development Research Centre (IDRC) on contractual basis. Recent projects for UNESCO include a comparative study of national information policies and strategies: the development of access to information in the public domain. Projects for IDRC include the formulation of a framework for the development of national environmental systems; and an in depth study of the impact of information on decision making.

— **Knowledge Forum :** The aim of FID's knowledge forum, which represents the collective expertise of FID individual members and specialized committees and special intercut groups, is to make this pool of knowledge available to FID's wider membership and to the international information community in general. The FID website is a key element of the knowledge forum, which also comprises FID's professional network its publications and meetings, the GTIA, and the project and activities of the committees and special interest groups.

— **Awards :** The Distinguished Information professional award is awarded biennially to honour and information professional with an outstanding track record. Dr. Shawky Salem training Grant for Arab Specialists in library and information sciences is managed jointly with the International Federation of Library Associations and Institution (IFLA) and awarded enable an expert in library science, who is a national of an Arab country, to attend the IFLA and FID conference in alternate years. Besides, the Ranganathan award for classification research is presented every two years.

— **Publications :** *FID Review* : In 1999, FID launched this new peer-reviewed journal which is published 6 times a year.

- FID Occasional Paper Series : Currently includes 16 papers dealing with key information issues
- FID Directory
- FID's Membership Directory
- FID's biennial conference proceedings.

In short, we can say, as one of the leading international professional organizations concerned with information work, FID will make these cross-cutting themes central to its future programme and aim to being into its membership young and committed professionals from the many disciplines which are also concerned these issues.

2. International Federation of Library Associations and Institutions (IFLA)

International Federation of Library Associations (IFLA) was founded in 1927 with the aim of promoting international cooperation and understanding among library associations and library professionals. It all started at the 50th Anniversary Conference of the Library Association (UK) held at Edinburgh when the "International Library and Bibliographical Committee" was formed. In 1929 the name was changed to "International Federation of Library Associations" and the expansion of the name to "International Federation of Library Associations and Institutions" was adopted in 1976. Today IFLA is represented in almost 146 countries all over the world.

(a) Objectives : The broad objectives of IFLA are :

(i) to serve as a body through which librarianship can be represented in matters of international interest;

(ii) to support and coordinates research and studies through its global network of information professionals; and

(iii) to cooperate with other international organizations in the field of information, documentation and archives.

(b) Organization : The membership is of two kinds : (i) full membership, which is admitted by the Executive Board to library associations or national and international associations or organizations with similar interest, and (ii) Associate membership, which is open to libraries, bibliographical institutes and similar institutions. No voting rights, admitted by the secretariat.

As far as the structure is concerned, it consists of following :

General Council : The General Council consists of the members of the Executive Board and of the representatives nominated by the member associations of IFLA. General Council Meetings are held annually and are visited by about 800 persons.

Executive Board : The Executive Board consists of the President, six Vice-presidents and the Treasurer. It is elected by the General Council on proposal by the Consultative Committee. The election is for 3 years with a possible re-election for one more term.

Consultative Committee : The Consultative Committee is an advisory body, consisting of the members of the Executive Board, the chairmen and secretaries of sections, committees, and international full members.

Programme Development Group : IFLA Programme Development Group was established in 1969 as an advisory body for the Executive Board on professional problems. The members are appointed by the Consultative Committee for 3 years with re-election possible for another 3 years.

Sections and Committees : The professional work of IFLA is concentrated in sections and committees. In 1973, the following sections and committees were active in IFLA.

Sections and Sub-sections : National and University Libraries, University Libraries, Public Libraries, Library Work with Children, Libraries in Hospitals, Special Libraries, Observatory Libraries, Social Science Libraries, Parliamentary Libraries, Administrative Libraries, School Libraries and Library Schools.

Committees : Cataloguing, International Leading, Exchange of Publications, Official Publications, Periodicals and Serial Publications, Statistics and Standardization, Rare and Precious Books, Library Buildings, Mechanization, Bibliography, Library Theory and Research.

Working Groups : The following working groups are actively contributing to achieve the objective of IFLA.

— Working Group on Developing Countries.

— Working Group on Research and Development in Documentation and Librarianship.

(c) Activities : The activities of association include :

— **Core Programmes:** The interests and concerns shared by all libraries, librarians and their users intersect in the activities of the IFLA Core Programmes. The objectives and projects of the core programmes relate to those of the divisions and sections. The core programmes comprise of current and internationally relevant issues such as Preservation and Conservation (PAC), Universal Availability of Publications (UAP), Universal Bibliographic Control and International MARC (UBCIM), and Universal Dataflow and Telecommunications (UDT). IFLA's fifth Core Programme, Advancement of Librarianship (ALP) covers as wide spectrum of IFLA's Activities, but is also very mission oriented by concentrating on issues specific to developing counties.

— **UAP-Universal Availability of Publications:** It is both an objective and programme. The objective is the widest possible availability of published material to intending users, wherever and whenever they need it and in the format required. Published materials include not only printed materials, but audio-visual materials and publications recorded in electronic form. The programme aims to improve availability at all levels, from the local to the international, and all stages, from the publication of new material to the retention of last copies, both by positive action and by the removal of barriers. It aims to ensure that improved access to information on publications is matched by improved access to the publications themselves.

The office is also the IFLA office for International Lending, which aim, to further and improve international lending by :

- Giving practical support to those who are engaged in international lending.
- Collecting and publicizing information of interest to those concerned with international lending.
- Conducting and encouraging research and study of relevance to international lending

— **PAC- Preservation and Conservation :** IFLA core programme on Preservation and Conservation (PAC) was officially created during the IFLA annual coherence in Nairobi in 1984 to focus efforts on issues of preservation and initiate worldwide cooperation for the preservation of library materials, but the PAC programme was effectively launched in Vienna during the 1986 conference on the Preservation of Library Materials sponsored by the Conference of Directors of national Libraries, with IFLA and UNESCO.

PAC has been originally conceived in decentralized way as a Focal Point to manage activities and Regional Centers responsible for their choices and policies. The Focal Point which is an International Centre has been hosted by the Bibliotheque National in Paris since 1992. There are 6 Regional Centres respectively located in Washington, Caracas, Tokyo, Canberra and Moscow. The International centre in Paris acts as the Regional Centre Western Europe, Middle East and Africa.

The International Centre and the Regional Centres are linked by a network. Each centre is independent and acts according to the preoccupations identified in its geographical area. Its main duty is to agree with the objectives of PAC core Programme and to maintain cooperation with other centres through specific activities. The Directors meet regularly for working sessions to define the orientations of the programme.

— **ISBDs :** IFLA developed and published in 1974 the International Standard Bibliographic Description for Monographic Publications ISBD(M) as the basis for rules of description of monographic materials in AACR-2. In 1975, IFLA and the Joint Steering Committee for the Revision for AACR (JSC/AACR) jointly developed the General International Standard Bibliographic Description ISBD(G). It serves as a frame work for the description of all types of publication, in different media ensuring uniform approach in bibliographic description.

— **Publications :** In the monograph series IFLA has broughtout a number of useful publications. In addition, following periodical publications are published;

- *IFLA Journal* (Quarterly);
- *International Cataloguing* (Quarterly);
- *IFLA Annual*;
- *IFLA Directory* (Annual); and
- *IFLA News*

— **IFLA Fellowships, Funds and Grants :** IFLA also administers a number of grants and scholarships to enable aspiring library and information professionals from all over the world to enhance their training and to provide funding for new and exiting projects in the field of librarianship.

10

Activities of UGC and UNESCO

Q. : What is University Grants Commission (UGC)? Discuss its role in promoting Library Services.

or

Explain the role of the University Grants Commission in the development of libraries.

Ans. : University Grants Commission (UGC) is a statutory organization established by an Act of Parliament in 1956. This is a national body for the co-ordination, determination and maintenance of standards of university education. The UGC serves as a vital link between the union and state governments and the institutions of higher learning. In addition to its role of giving grants to universities and colleges, the UGC also advises union and state governments on the measures necessary for the improvement of university education. It also frames regulations such as those on the minimum standards of instruction and qualifications of teachers on the advice of subject specialists and academicians with whom it frequently interacts in connection with the formulation, evaluation and monitoring of programmes.

The Commission, being an apex body in maintaining higher education in the country, is playing a major role in promoting library and information services in these universities and colleges. Besides, it has also established and constituted a number of libraries/information centers/study centers and committees to provide quality education and service in the field of library and information activities. Some of these are :

(i) Financial Assistance to University and College Libraries.

(ii) Curriculum Development Committee (CDC) on Library & Information Science.

(iii) Establishment of National Information Centres.

(iv) Establishment of INFLIBNET.

(v) Modernization of university libraries, and

(vi) National Review Committee on University and College Libraries.

(i) Financial Assistance to University and College Libraries

Financial assistance is given to universities and colleges including Central Universities, State Universities, Deemed Universities and Government and affiliated colleges, which receive grants for building up libraries so as to meet the demands of the students, teachers and research scholars. The Commission provides substantial grants for the acquisition of books and journals.

For other infrastructural facilities also like library buildings, furniture and equipment grants arc given in every five-year plan period. It also introduced a scheme of 'book bank' in colleges and universities by providing grants to acquire multiple copies of costly text books recommended in all the disciplines. The objective of this scheme was to provide text books to poor, needy and deserving students for home study on long term basis by charging nominal deposits. This Scheme is no longer in operation by UGC support.

(ii) Curriculum Development Committee (CDC) on Library and Information Science

The UGC constituted CDC on Library and Information Science in 1990 to restructure the courses of studies. The committee in its recommendations framed guidelines for LIS schools, covering admission policy, students and faculty strength, instructional methodology, teaching aids and application of information technology etc. Besides, it also constituted a committee called UGC Panel in Library and Information Science to suggest the changes to be brought in the education and training of LIS courses.

(iii) Establishment of National Information Centres

The objective of establishing National Information Centres in specialized areas is to provide improved access to information and to provide bibliographic support to teachers and research scholars in their respective fields. Three such centers, have been established and they have developed computer databases to render reference and information services, documentation services and current awareness services.

(iv) Establishment of INFLIBNET

The UGC established an Information and Library Network (INFLIBNET) Programme with headquarters at Ahemadabad as a project of the Inter University Centre for Astronomy and Astrophysics (IUCA), Pune in April 1991. The INFLIBNET Programme aims at the establishment of a national network of libraries and information centers in institutions of higher learning including universities, colleges, R & D institutions and national organizations like CSIR, ICMR, ICSSR, ICAR, DOE, etc,

It is a computer-communication network of libraries and bibliographical information centres, and is a co-operative network programme for pooling, sharing and optimisation of resources, facilities and services of libraries and information centres, in the university system as well as in the R & D complex. It provides access to information to students, academics and researchers in rendering various information and documentation services such as (a) catalogue-based service (b) database service (e) document delivery service (d) collection development and (e) communication-based service.

(v) Modernization of University Libraries

Recent advances in information and communication technology and its utility have forced the university libraries to computerize their services and connecting themselves to various network programmes like INFLIBNET so as to provide fast, efficient and reliable computerized information service to its users. The UGC has also provided special financial assistance to central university libraries and other university libraries established during last few financial years for updating their library facilities. The main objective was to computerize their library activities and connect them to INFLIBNET programmes. The utilization of the fund provided for the purpose is to meet the following expenses.

(a) Purchase of computer system, monitor, printer, terminals, software etc.

(b) Computer, furniture and electrical fitting and air-conditioning.

(c) Mode, telephone line and connection to nearest communication mode.

(d) Appointment of Information Scientist.

(e) Support for Data Entry Work.

(f) Purchase of books, journals, Audio-visuals and their processing.

(g) Data Entry conversion (modernisation).

(h) Staff training, and

(i) Other contingencies etc.

(vi) National Review Committee on University and College Libraries

The purpose of constituting such a committee is to review the utilization of grants to central universities and some state university libraries of Rs. 2 crores and Rs.50 lakhs respectively, secondly, to prepare a status report of university and college libraries in India, and, thirdly to prepare a strategy plan/guidelines for the future for smooth functioning of these university and college libraries.

Recently, UGC in 2003 took a big decision to implement UGC-INFONET programme. In this programme, each university will be provided Internet Connectivity through various modes e.g. VSAT Link, Radio Link or Satelite Link etc. depending upon the geographical conditions of the university where it is situated. After linking, free access to e-journals will be provided to them. This will be a big change in the library services. Some of the universities have already been provided this facility and rest are in the development phase.

Q. : Give an account on the role of UNESCO in developing library, documentation and information activities.

or

Discuss the activities of UNESCO in developing library services.

Ans. : UNESCO was founded in 1946, by an inter-governmental agency belonging to the United Nations system. Among many subjects implied in the title, it deals with Library, Documentation, Information, Archives, Book Production, Copyright and similar other things. These subjects are handled at the UNESCO headquarters by different units. However, in 1976, two main divisions, namely that of Documentation and Information which has been responsible for carrying out the UNISIST programme were combined to establish a new division known as the General Information Programme (PGI). The operational information services within UNESCO such as Documentation Systems Division including Computerised Documentation services, UNESCO Library and UNESCO Archives are administratively separated from the PGI. It is learnt that very recently, the PGI and the operational services divisions have been grouped together as General Information Service under a unified command.

(a) Objectives

The objectives are : contributing to the world peace, security and international understanding by promoting education, science and culture among the nations of the world; fostering respect for justice, rule of the law and basic freedoms for all people; giving momentum to developmental activities in the member-states through operational assistance. The UNESCO seeks to create a new world order by realizing its objectives.

(b) Organisational Structure

It has at present 157 members and one associate member in the organization with its headquarters situated in Paris. The organization consists of a General Conference, an Executive Board, a Secretariat Co-operating Bodies and Regional Offices.

(c) Activities

UNESCO activities in developing library, documentation and information activities are grouped into following directions:

(i) Principles and Structure of Documentation, Library and Archives services : UNESCO through its various principles has contributed a lot to documentation, library and archival services. The UNESCO Public Library Manifesto gave a new image and wide scope to public libraries. It influenced the development of public libraries in many member states and underdeveloped countries and recognized the role of libraries in educating communities.

UNESCO also concerned itself with school libraries and educational documentation services both as an essential aid to education and an ideal means of establishing the learning and reading habit among different groups of people. Concerning the university the special libraries, UNESCO initiated several activities like seminars, technical assistance, missions, grants, publications, etc. to improve the services of libraries in member states. UNESCO's contribution to the development of scientific and technical documentation centers helped member countries to overcome problems of information explosion and paved the way for the increase of S & T research. UNESCO also recommended to member countries the selling up of a National System (NATIS) which helped to lay the foundation of national, regional and international cooperation in information services.

(ii) Internationalization of Documentation, Library and Archival Services : UNESCO has contributed to a great extent in the internationalization of documentation, library and archival services at national, regional and International levels. It helped in the free flow of information and documentation embodying the product of the human intellect. Its periodic associations with international non-governmental organisations like FID, IFLA, and ICA have enabled it to extend its programme of activities. Many international seminars, workshops, conferences, courses, have been organized throughout the world.

(iii) Professional Training : Through the initiative of UNESCO, the International Institute for Educational Planning started teaching its regular students on the planning of library service.

UNESCO's action in this field takes the form of meetings of experts, specialized courses, the setting up of regional training centres like those in Dakar (Senegal), Kampala (Uganda), Legon (Ghana) and Kingston (Jamaica), and schools of librarianship, the sending of experts and consultants to member-states, the granting of fellowships and the organizing of courses for teachers in schools for librarians and archivists. These programmes have contributed to the improvement of the courses given in these schools and to the opening of additional schools and have helped in creating awareness of the fact that the improvement of library services is hampered if governments do not give priority to the training of librarians, documentalists and archivists. UNESCO also considered that the professional training of librarians and specialists in the information sciences would be incomplete unless interest in research was stimulated as part of such training so that trainees would have a wider-outlook and real professional aptitude. For this purpose the Organization helped to set up library research centres, one in the school of librarianship of the University of Dakar and one in the Department of Information Sciences of the Faculty of Arts at the University of Buenos Aires.

It also supported several training programmes, library schools, international summer schools, etc. to create well trained library personnel.

(iv) Establishment of Public, University and National Libraries : The UNESCO championed the cause of Public Library movement in the Third World. Its faith in Public Libraries as means of continuing education and cradle of democracies, providing objective knowledge and information without any restrictions, is reflected in its publication 'UNESCO Public Library Manifesto' (1949, revised in 1972 and 1994). It established Pilot Public Libraries in Enugu (Nigeria), Medellin (Columbia) and New Delhi (India). It conducted several regional seminars at Brazil, Lebanon, Nigeria, and India with the support of the member-states on the theme of public libraries including the Regional Seminar on 'Library Development in Asia' in 1960.

(v) UNISIST and NATIS : NATIS, the concept of a national information and library system; and UNISIST, the concept of an international system for the transfer of information, together constitute UNESCO's greatest contribution in the field, with which helping to place documentation, library and archives services upon national, regional and international foundations become possible. The goals, scope and purposes of NATIS and UNISIST had been approved by the UNESCO General Conference at different sessions and the principles underlying them were the organization's response to the growing, complex and pressing problem of how to bring the bibliographical and documentary resources of mankind within the reach of everyone all over the world without limitations of any kind.

(vi) NWICO (New World Information and Communication Order) : The UNESCO is helping the developing countries to strengthen their communication systems by its programmes of New World Information and Communication Order (NWICO) and the Inter-governmental Programmes for the Development of Communication (IPDC). With an intention of promoting regional co-operation, better understanding and socio-economic development in Asia and the Pacific regions, UNESCO established in 1984 a Regional Network for Exchange of Information and Experience in Science and Technology in Asia and the Pacific (ASTINFO), Later in 1986 another network called Asia-Pacific Information Network in Social Sciences (APINESS) was established.

(vii) ISORID (International Information Systems in Research in Documentation) : UNESCO has also established an International Information System on Research in Documentation (ISORID) for collecting and dissemination of information on research activities in documentation, libraries and archives conducted at different institutions all over the world. The establishment of clearing house for handling information on science and information policies of the countries of the world under the programme of Science and Technology Policies Information Exchange System (SPINES) has also been developed. It also developed databases and information systems such as the Data Retrieval system for Documentation in the Social and Human Sciences (DARE) and the International Bureau of Education Documentation and Information system (IBEDOC).

(viii) Book Promotion : A familiar problem in most of the developing countries is lack of books in their vernacular languages. UNESCO, has organized a number of regional meetings to study this problem and as a result regional book promotion centers have come up with the participation of member states.

(iv) Publications : The following are a few important publications of the UNESCO:

1. *Copyright Bulletin* (Quarterly)
2. *Impact of Science on Society* (Quarterly)
3. *UNESCO Courier* (Monthly)
4. *UNESCO Journal of Information Science, Librarianship and Archives Administration* (Quarterly) [Formerly *UNESCO Bulletin for Libraries*]
5. *UNISIST News letter* (Quarterly)
6. *World Guide to Library Schools and Training Course's in Documentation,* 1981
7. *UNESCO Chronicle* (Monthly)

As far as UNESCO contribution in Indian context is concerned, India has been a member for the UNESCO from the very beginning. The Delhi Public Library was established in India with its assistance only. UNESCO helped us a lot by undertaking many projects in our country conducting training programmes, seminars and providing technical expertise.

While the Indian National Commission for UNESCO is the official agency, the NISSAT (National Information System for Science and Technology) in the DSIR (Department of Scientific and Industrial Research) is the focal point for UNISIST/PGI (General Information Programme of UNESCO and is also the Coordinating Centre for ASTINFO Programme.

UNESCO is also supporting APINESS Programme for which NASSDOC (of ICSSR) is the focal point.

India has also organized a few conferences and Regional Seminars of UNESCO. Important among them are:

— Ninth General Conference (Delhi) (1956).

— Regional Seminar on Book Distribution, Promotion and Market Research (Delhi) (1959).

— Regional Seminar on Libraries in South-Asia (1960).

— Metropolitan Libraries Seminar (Delhi) (1973).

— Seminar on Handling and Retrieval of Chemical Information (Delhi) (1986)

Concluding, it is seen that the efforts of UNESCO have increased considerably in promoting international co-operation and more stress is also given in the application of computers and communication technologies in the development of information systems. The other activities of UNESCO aim at improving national and regional programmes such as training, seminars, refresher courses, in service training to managers, etc.

11
Miscellaneous

Q. : Discuss in brief the activities of some of the information systems and networks in the field of library science.

Ans. : In India and at the international level various information centres, systems and networks are established which are working for the betterment and upliftment of the library activities. These systems and networks are now the need of the days in view the fastly changing information environment. So, large number of libraries and information centres of today fare willing to cooperate and coordinate through Information System and Networks, keeping in view their ability to minimise the duplication and maximise the utilization of financial resources and the ease with which the resources of the participants can be made assessable to anyone, anywhere and at any point of time. Some of them are briefly discussed here.

1. AGRIS (Information System on Agricultural Sciences and Technology)

AGRIS, a cooperative world agricultural information system, in which some 114 countries and 14 international institutions are at present participating, became operational in 1975. It is sponsored by the Food and Agricultural Organization of UN. The input in standard format is provided by participating countries. It uses common computer configuration and software packages located at the IAEA, Vienna. The information processed through computer yields two output products every month, namely printed AGRINDEX and AGRIS magnetic tape. These services contain full bibliographical descriptions of all documents and offer facility to retrieve information from AGRIS database which now exceeds 12 million entries in 16 main subjects under 85 subject categories and 817 commodities. The annual addition to the database is around 1.2 lakh items.

The AGRIS database is being maintained online by a number

of international data centres, such as DIALOG, IAEA and ESA. AGRIS Database is available to national centres on magnetic tapes. Though abstracts of articles are not printed in AGRINDEX, rather they are available on magnetic tapes and in microfiches. Cumulative indexes to AGRINDEX are produced annually in microfiche.

With the Agricultural Research Information Centre of ICAR, as the national centre, India has also been participating in the AGRIS programme. On as average, 3,500 bibliographical entries are passed on to AGRIS database as Indian input every year. The Agricultural Research Information centre receives from FAO every month updated AGRIS magnetic tape. A computerised SDI service is operational using Burrough's B-4700 computer systems of the Indian Agricultural Statistics Research Institute. A retrieval programme has also been developed for carrying out retrospective search. The SDI service is at present offered against 200 profiles.

AGRIS is now firmly established as a single comprehensive current inventory of world wide agricultural literature and meets the information needs of agricultural scientists and others.

2. INIS (International Nuclear Information System)

INIS, is sponsored by the International Atomic Energy Agency, Vienna, started functioning since 1970. It is a practical example of how international cooperation in the development of computer-based information system can be achieved. All the member states of IAEA are participants in the cooperative venture of bibliographical control of world's nuclear science and literature. INIS has the objective of achieving maximum economy in time, money and effort and avoiding duplication in handling nuclear science literature. The salient features of INIS are international IR system, cooperative venture communication with participants, maximum decentralization and minimum centralization, adherence to standards and rules, computer-based systems, a document retrieval system, use of thesaurus for subject indexing, indexing and abstracting service with a high quality input, a dynamic and flexible system, machine readable information service, and a mission-oriented system.

A designated centre in each participating country is responsible for identification and selection of documents of its origin and preparation of their bibliographical description in a standardized form by categorizing, cataloguing, indexing and abstracting and also making available one copy of the piece of literature which can not be obtained through normal publication channels. It has developed its own thesaurus for subject indexing. The input so received is checked, corrected and transferred into machine-readable form at INIS headquarters, where access to a large computer system is available. The merged input after computer processing produces an output in magnetic tapes, constituting a secondary service/ database for current nuclear science literature. Besides, printed INIS Atomindex is also brought out. The INIS Atomindex on magnetic tapes received from the headquarters by the national centres is used for offering current awareness, SDI service, etc, according to local inforamtion needs. The national centre can also obtain from INIS copies of any source documents, whenever required.

India has been actively participating in INIS from the beginning. The library and information services division of the Bhabha Atomic Research Centre, Mumbai, is the national centre responsible for INIS activities. It has been successfully performing its tasks of inputting and output utilization. On account of participation in INIS, Indian scientists have no longer any problem in having access to world's nuclear science literature.

3. NISSAT (National Information System in Science & Technology)

NISSAT came to be established as a project of Science and Technology Plan in the Fifth Year Plan. In was authorized for implementation in June 1977 by the Department of Science and Technology, India. Its broad objectives are coordination, interlinking, filling up gaps, strengthening infrastructures, standardizatioin, etc. with regard to information sources and services. Its developmental and short term objectives are all directed towards improving national capability in information collection, handling and service, by taking up a number of measures. The NISSAT network consists of (1) sectorial system, (2) regional system, and (3) other specialized services. It is not an operational system directly performing information functions, but it plays an advisory and promotional role. Its activities are expected to have catalytic and multiplier effect.

(i) Aims and Objectives

The NISSAT have following aims and objectives :-

— to help the country in developing, generating, processing and disseminating the information;

— to assist in optimizing the usage of existing library and information systems and develop new ones;

— to enhance the coordination and cooperation at the regional, national and international levels in the areas in Information services and system;

— to facilitate education and training in the field of Information science and technology; and

— to participate and assist others in carrying research activities in the field of information services and technology to bring upon improvements in the existing information services and system.

(ii) Activities:

Some of the major activities of NISSAT are:

(a) Online Services : In order to provide current information for the assistance of scientists and technologists, the NISSAT has introduced the facility of online information through the five Centres at Bangalore, Kolkata, Chennai, New Delhi, and Pune. These Centres are addressed as National Access Centres to Information Databases - NACIDS. Besides Selective Dissemination of Information (SDI) service is also provide to user as per their profiles.

(b) Initiation of Library Networks : Metropolitan Library Networks have also been initiated by NISSAT. It has launched:-

Calcutta Library Network (CALIBNET)

Delhi Library Network (DELINET)

(c) Assistance in Computerised Processing of Information : Keeping in view each kind of library's requirement for the computerized processing of information, NISSAT has acquired proven version of Software packages like CDS/ISIS Mini - micro Version, SUPERDOC and IDAMS from UNESCO. The NISSAT also has official rights for the distribution of CDS/ISIS in India on the behalf of UNESCO.

(d) Professional Training to Library and Information Professionals : The NISSAT has also taken initiative in the field of education and training of professionals in the field of Library and Information Science at it's educational outlets at the INSDOC, New Delhi, DRTC, Bangalore; RCC, Calcutta, and University of Poona, Pune. Besides NISSAT for the UNESCO has also prepared the standard course material for library and information science.

(e) International Cooperation : NISSAT is a regular participant in the activities of ASTINEO/ UNESCO programmes.

Besides, there are a number of Documentation Centres in India, which are providing some of the services that of an National Information System. The most prominent among them are:

INSDOC, DESIDOC and NASSDOC

4. Indian National Scientific Documentation Centre (INSDOC)

INSDOC, established in 1952, by the Council of Scientific and Industrial Research, with UNESCO's technical assistance, is a premier national level information centre, devoted to all branches of science and technology. With well developed resources and facilities, it has a distinguished record of service and performance in serving the scientific community with bibliographical information support. Over the years, it has grown in size and in its range of activities and has built up a body of expertise in scientific information. In 1963, INSDOC emerged as an Independent Institute with its own Executive Council and Director.

(a) Objectives : The Objectives of INSDOC since its inception are :

- to act as a repository of periodical collection pertaining to areas of Science, Technology and Engineering;
- to provide Selective Dissemination of Information (SDI) Services;
- to provide answers to the Reference Queries;
- to provide Translation services;
- to act as a depository for National output in Science, Technology and Engineering.
- to cooperate with other Documentation Centres in different areas at the National and International levels.

(b) Activities : The INSDOC's objectives have been carried through the activities as follows :

- It is the leading S & T database producer in India.
- For India, INSDOC acts as a host to the provision of online databases.
- It is the most significant institute in the area of S & T which provides, consultations to the S & T people in India.

— It also acts as S & T repository for India.

— INSDOC also offers training in the area of Information Science and Technology, besides two year course in Associateship in Library Science.

(c) Services : The Services offered by INSDOC include :

— Online and CD-ROM based bibliographical informational retrieval.

— Networking Services and Developing Bibliometric Analysis.

— Human Resource Development in Information Science & Technology.

— Translation from foreign languages to English.

— Document copy supply.

— Microforms and Reprography.

— Desktop Publishing (DTP)

— Cover Designing

— Printing

(d) Publications : It publishes following publications :

— **Indian Science Abstracts (semi-monthly) :** It is a national abstracting service in science and technology, reporting annually about 25,000 scientific documents on the work done in India.

— **National Index of Translations (monthly) :** Listing about 250 translations every month produced by about 25 R & D institutions in the country.

— **Contents List of Soviet Scientific Periodicals (monthly) :** Reproducing English contents pages of about 250 Russian scientific periodicals.

— **Accession List of Russian Scientific Publications (bi-monthly)** Listing in each issue about 300 Russian books received from USSR under a collaborative agreement.

— **Annals of Library Science and Information Studies (quarterly) :** It is primary journal carrying original and review articles and others.

Recently, in 2002 INSDOC has been merged with NISCOM (National Institute of Science and Communication) and is known by the name NISCAIR, the National Institute of Science Communication and Information Resources.

5. Defence Science Information and Documentation Centre (DESIDOC)

DESIDOC was established in 1958 under the Defence Research and Development Organisation (DRDO) to serve primarily the information requirements of DRDO scientists. In 1967, it became an independent institution under DRDO. It functions as a central agency in DRDO to collect scientific and technical information from various user groups in the defence establishments. It has also a coordination role in the information set-up of DRDO.

The Defence Science Library of DESIDOC has built up an active collection of publications of interest to defence science which is multi-disciplinary. It has some 1.40 lakh items in stock comprising 40,000 books, 40,000 reports, 14,000 back volumes of periodicals and others. It receives about 800 current periodicals.

(a) Activities : The main activities of DESIDOC are as under :

(i) It offers a number of services to its users. SDI service was being offered until recently by manual method to senior officials of DRDO and Ministry of Defence. A computer-aided SDI service is now being operated against some limited profiles, which is to be enlarged progressively. It brings out a bi-monthly Patents Information Alerts to draw the attention of scientist to Indian and foreign patents of their subject interest and Defence Reports Abstracts covering NASA, NTIS, RAND, DRIC and other report literature. The bi-monthly indexing service called DESIDOC list, is a current awareness publication. It has also brought out at least six state-of-the-art reports in recent years. It also undertakes literature search and supplied bibliographies on specific subjects. Besides, DESIDOC is also compiling a union catalogue of periodicals in DRDO libraries.

(ii) It has in-house translation facilities for some foreign languages. It maintains also a translation bank. English abstracts of foreign language scientific articles of interest to DRDO are prepared and circulated to defence scientists.

(iii) It has been engaged in computer based information activities. It is offering computer based SDI service, which is to be expanded. It has been maintaining its databases in machine readable from. It is now planning to set up DRDO Information Retrieval System, covering libraries/TICs of DRDO establishments.

(iv) It has a good range of reprography and audio-visual equipment and in-house printing facilities.

(b) Training Programmes : It also organizes, from time to time, short term training courses in different areas of information science for the benefit of DRDO information personnel. It also offers technical advice and consultancy in library, documentation and information fields.

(c) Publications :

— *Defence Science Journal* (quarterly)

— *R & D Bulletin* (quarterly)

— *R & D Digest* (bi-monthly)

— *Popular Science and Technology* (half-yearly)

— *DRDC Newsletter* (monthly)

— *DESIDOC Bulletin of Information Technology* (bi-monthly).

Besides, DESIDOC arranges some seminars and short-term training courses time to time. In 1986, a national seminar was held and as a result of its recommendations, it has taken measures to evolve a Defence Science Information System for the country.

6. National Social Science Documentation Centre (NASSDOC)

National Social Science Documentation Centre (NASSDOC), renamed so in 1985, was established in 1970 by the Indian Council of Social Science Research, New Delhi, with the object of providing information support to social science research activities in the country. It is well equipped with resources and facilities and has been carrying out a number of useful programmes and projects.

The main objectives of NASSDOC have been to bring out the Union Catalogues of Social Science Periodicals and Serials. These are brought out in 3 series :

(i) Union Catalogue of Social Science Periodicals;

(ii) Union Catalogue of Social Science Serials;

(iii) Current list of Social Science Periodicals.

Besides, it has many other publications including :

(i) Inter Library Resource Centre holding list;

(ii) Periodicals in NASSDOC; A current list etc.

Services Offered by NASSDOC : Some of the important services of NASSDOC include :

(a) Bibliographic Services : NASSDOC has an impressive record of bibliography compilation work. Under its Research Information Service, it brings out subject, area study and language bibliographies. Bibliographies on Student Teaching, and Social Sciences in the Present Day World are some recent subject bibliographies. While work on some states in regard to area study bibliography has been completed, it is in progress in the case of others. About 10,000 titles in English and regional languages have been collected under the area study project. In the language bibliography, compilation work in Gujarati, Hindi, Kannada and Oriya is in progress. It is presently engaged in bringing out Index to Indian Periodicals; Sociology and Psychology (1915-70), which is a retrospective cumulative index.

(b) Reference and Referral Services : Like other Documentation Centres, reference as well as referral service is also offered by the NASSDOC. It provides document delivery support by supplying photocopies of individual papers to research workers. It has printing facilities on a small documentation centres for compilation of indexes, bibliographies, etc.

(c) Consultancy Service : NASSDOC also offers consultancy and advisory services in social sciences documentation and information. Recently, it has also started training programmes in social science documentation.

(d) National and International Cooperation : It undertakes exchange programme with various national and international organization and also collaborates in context of bibliographical control in Social Science.

(e) Publications : Some of the publications of NASSDOC are listed below :

(i) Current Contents to Indian Social Science Journals (Quarterly)

(ii) Conference alert (Quarterly)

(iii) Acquisition Update (Bi-annual)

(iv) Bibliographic Reprint (Irregular)

(v) APINESS Newsletter (Bi-annual)

(vi) Aged in India : An Annotated Bibliography

(vii) Bibliography on India in 2000 A.D. (with abstracts).

Q. : Write short notes on the followings :

1. **Freedom of Access of Information**
2. **Universal Availability of Publications (UAP)**
3. **Copy right**
4. **Data Centres**
5. **Information Analysis Centre**
6. **Information Dissemination Centre**

Ans. :

1. Freedom of access to Information

Libraries have been the traditional preservers of recorded information. With the spread of democracy in most parts of the world, libraries have remained the primary sources of access to recorded information. Evolution of the Internet has thrown open opportunities on the one hand, while has posed some challenges, and freedom of access to information to public is threatened by the commercial, political and other interests.

Freedom of Access to Information and Freedom of Expression (FAIEF) is one of the core activities of IFLA. FAIFE which came into existence in 1997, defends and promotes the basic human rights defined in Article 19 of the United Nations Universal Declaration of Human Rights. It monitors the state of intellectual freedom within the library community worldwide, supports IFLA policy development and cooperation with other international human rights organizations and responds of IFLA's behalf to violation of principles.

IFLA Statement on Freedom

The statement was prepared by IFLA/FAIFE and approved by the Executive Board of IFLA 25 March 1999, at the Hugue, Neitherlands. International Federation of Library Associations and Institutions supports defends and promotes intellectual freedom as defined in the United Nations Universal Declaration of Human Rights. It declares that human beings have a fundamental right to access to expressions of knowledge, creative thought and intellectual activity, and to express their views publicly. It believes that the right to know and freedom of expression are two aspects of the same principle. The right to know is a requirement for freedom of thought and conscience; freedom of thought and freedom of expression are necessary conditions for freedom of access to information.

IFLA asserts that a commitment to intellectual freedom is a core responsibility for the library and information profession. Therefore, it calls upon libraries and library staff to adhere to the principles of intellectual freedom, uninhibited access to information and freedom of expression and to recognize the privacy of library user. IFLA urges its members actively to promote the acceptance and realization of these principles. In doing so, IFLA affirms that :

— Libraries provide access to information, ideas and works of imagination. They serve as gateways to knowledge, thought and culture.

— Libraries provide essential support for lifelong learning, independent decision-making and cultural development for both individuals and groups.

— Libraries contribute to the development and maintenance of intellectual freedom and help to safeguard basic democratic values and universal civil rights.

— Libraries have a responsibility both to guarantee and to facilitate access to expressions of knowledge and intellectual activity. To this end, libraries shall acquire, preserve and make available the widest variety of materials, reflecting the plurality and diversity of society.

— Libraries shall ensure that the selection and availability of library materials and services is governed by professional considerations and not by political, moral and religious views.

— Libraries shall acquire, organize and disseminate information freely and oppose any form of censorship.

— Libraries shall make materials, facilities and services equally accessible to all users. There shall be no discrimination due to race, creed, gender, age or for any other reason.

— Library users shall have the right to personal privacy and anonymity. Librarians and other library staff shall not disclose the identity of users or the materials they use to a third party.

— Libraries funded from public sources and to which the public have access shall uphold the principles of intellectual freedom.

— Librarians and other employees in such libraries have a duty to uphold those principles.

— Librarians and other professional libraries staff snail fulfil their responsibilities both to their employer and to their uses. In cases of conflict between those responsibilities, the duty towards the user shall take precedence.

2. Universal Availability of Publications (UAP)

UAP is one of the core programmes of International Federation of Library Associations and Institutions (IFLA). UAP is also an objective of IFLA for "widest possible availability of published material that is, recorded knowledge issued for public use, to intending users, wherever and whenever they need it in the format required. Published materials include not only printed materials, including so-called 'grey literature', but also audio-visual material and publications recorded in electronic form. To work towards this objective, the programme aims to improve availability at ail levels, from the local to the international, and at all stages, from the publication of new material to the retention of last copies, both by positive action and by the removal of barriers, UAP aims to ensure that improved, access to information on publications is matched by improved access to publications themselves.

For this purpose, IFLA has set up its office for UAP and international lending at the British Library, Boston Spa, Wetherby, W Yorkshire, UK. This office aims to further and improve international lending by:

— giving practical support to those who are engaged in international lending.

— collecting and publicizing information of interest to those concerned with international lending.

— conducting and encouraging research and study of relevance to international lending.

— administering the International Lending Voucher Scheme.

The Publications of the UAP are :

— Model National Interlibrary Loan Code.

— Interlending and Document Delivery : principles and guidelines for procedure.

— UAP Newsletter.
— National Libraries of the World : an Address List.
— IFLA Fax Guidelines.
— Directory of Union Catalogues — a keyword searchable index.
— IFLA Guidelines for sending ILL requests by e-mail.
— Recommendations for Interlibrary Loan Response Codes.

3. Copy right

Copyright is the right over the presentation of idea in the written/recorded form, and not over the idea itself. It is a legal means of protecting the rights of the author of an original work, on the presumption that the work is a piece of property. Three important words have been specially discussed here : author work, and original. Broadly, author means the person who is the creator of the work and the work being a literary work or more appropriately as a written and graphic works, and the idea of "originality" is based on the existence of a direct link between the author's conception and judgement and the work which is created.

In simple terms, this means that what is protected, is the words which the author uses, not the information which those words convey or the ideas which they express. Librarianship and information work intersects with the copyright law. Therefore, it becomes essential for library and information professionals to know about the copyright and copyright law.

Copyright is not a right over an idea or thought, but over its publication in the written form and other forms e.g., audio-visual material. This can be illustrated in a simple way. Anybody can write about the ideas presented in a chapter, but the way of presentation, i.e., the use of words to describe copyright in another publication, should be different from the ones used in this publication. In case it is the same, it is violation of the copyright of this publication.

As libraries are forming cooperatives, and providing fee based services, and with globalization actually spreading across whole of the globe, understanding the concept of copyright and its laws, as far as these are concerned with providing library and information services, becomes essential for library and information professionals.

Copyright laws exist in almost all countries. At the international level, the Berne Convention (BC), with modifications of the 1886 treaty, and the Universal Copyright Convention (UCC), are the main protocols to which majority of the countries are party to UCC was worked out under the agencies of UNESCO. In present age, when information can be created, published, stored and disseminated in the electronic form, there are many changes have occurred. These changes are with regard to authorship, auditing, ease of copying, and responsibility for preservation.

IFLA supports the effective enforcement of copyright and recognizes that libraries have a crucial role to play in controlling as well as facilitating access to the increases number of local and remote electronic information resources. Librarians and information professionals promote respect for copyright and actively defend copyright works against piracy, unfair use and unauthorized exploitation, in both the print and the digital environment.

In order to maintain a balance between the interests of rights holders and users, IFLA has developed the following state of principles.

— In national copyright legislation, exceptions to copyright and related rights, allowed in the Berne Convention and endorsed by the WIPO treaties should be revised if necessary to ensure that permitted uses apply equally to information in electronic form and information in print.

— For copying over and above these provisions there should be administratively simple payment schemes.

— Temporary or technical copies which are incidental to the use of copyright material should be excluded from the scope of the reproduction right.

— For works in digital format without incurring a charge or seeking permission ail users of a library should be able to browse publicly available copyright material; read, listen to, or view publicly marketed copyright material privately, on site or remotely and copy, or have copied for them by library and information staff, a reasonable portion of a digital work in copyright for personal, educational or research use.

— Providing access to a digital format of a protected work to a user for a legitimate purpose such as research or study should be permitted under copyright law.

— The lending of published physical format digital materials by libraries should not be restricted by legislation.

— Contractual provisions, for example, within licensing arrangements, should not override reasonable lending of electronic resources by library staff.

— Legislation should give libraries and archives permission to convert copyright protected materials into digital format for preservation and conversation related purposes.

— Legislation should also cover the legal deposit of electronic media.

— National copyright legislation should render invalid any terms of a licence that restrict or override exceptions or limitations embodied in copyright law where the license is established unilaterally by the rightholders without the opportunity for negotiation of the terms of the license by the user.

— National copyright laws should aim for a balance between the rights of copyright owners to protect their interests through technical means and the rights of users to circumvent such measures for legitimate, non-infringing purposes.

— Copyright law should enunciate clear limitations on liability of third parties in circumstances where compliance cannot practically or reasonably be enforced.

In national copyright legislation, exceptions to copyright and related rights, allowed in the Berne Convention and endorsed by the WIPO (the World Intellectual Property Organization) treaties should be revised if necessary to ensure that permitted uses apply equally to information in electronic form and to information in print. The important points are :

— For copying over and above these provisions, there should be administratively simple payment schemes.

— Temporary or technical copies which are incidental to the use of copyright material should be excluded from the scope of the reproduction right?

— For works in digital format, without incurring a charge or seeking permission all users of a library should be able to :

  - browse publicly available copyright material;

- read, listen to, or view publicly marketed copyright material privately, on site or remotely:
- copy, or have copied for them by library and information staff a reasonable proportion of a digital work in copyright for personal, educational or research use.

Summing up, it can be said although, libraries as intermediaries have an important role to play in ensuring compliance with copyright law, liability should ultimately rest with the infringer.

4. Data Centres

The data centres are the organizations handling quantitative numerical or factual data, whose functions are to store collect, organize, analyse and disseminate data and provide various types of services on demand or in anticipation of demand. The services range from straight forward supply of data with reference to any query to correlation and critical compilation of data pertaining to any field of study, presented in a tabular or graphic form. Regular abstracts and indexes are produced by the data centres pertaining to different disciplines and made available in print or machine readable forms. There are various data centres operating at local, national and international levels.

5. Information Analysis Centres

An information analysis centre is a formally structured organizational unit, specifically established for the purpose of acquiring, storing, retrieving, evaluating, analysing, synthesizing, a body of information and/or data in a clearly defined specialized field. The purpose is to compile, repackage, organize and present pertinent information and/or data in a form most authoritative, timely and useful to a group of specialists.

The distinguishing characteristics of this type of centres, are as follows:

- The key activities of these centres are analysis, interpretation, synthesis, evaluation, and repackaging of information for the purpose of enabling users to assimilate the information or numerical data of a specific field.
- An information analysis centre uses subject specialists to perform the analysis, evaluation and synthesis.
- An information analysis centre produces new, evaluated

information in the form of critical services, state-of-art monographs or data compilations and usually provides substantive evaluated responses to queries.

— An information analysis centre provides assistance to a community of users and not just assistance to 'in-house' personnel.

— Information analysis centres provide the most user-oriented information service, in a timely, authoritative and evaluated form, that is convenient to the users.

6. Information Dissemination Centres

Information Dissemination Centres are those centres, whose primary function is to diffuse discipline-oriented information among its clientele. Such centres provide commercially available current awareness, selective dissemination and retrospective literature search services by searching computerized database. These centres may operate as units of organization that produce the data base or may be offering these services as independent organizations with proper connections with database generators,

These centres differ from the other type of information centres in their services are not geared to serve any specified group of users operating in any field or discipline, rather, they offer literature services to any group of specialist users, by searching any computerised database. These institutions are also known by the name information broker agencies, information consultants, etc. These trends are leading to development of information industries which have now started operating in many countries, offering services from simple document supply service to most complex information analysis and consolidation services, charging a fee for such services.

The Information dissemination centres, most of them being commercial organizations, have introduced an element of trade in the field of information services. Information marketing has thus, become a subject of great interest and attention is given to economies of information with reference to buying and selling information products and services.